MAKING
GLOBAL
DEALS

Jeswald W. Salacuse

MAKING
GLOBAL
DEALS

What Every Executive
Should Know About
Negotiating Abroad

Books are available at special discounts for bulk purchases (100 copies or more) for
sales promotions or premiums. Special editions, including personalized covers,
excerpts and corporate imprints can be created in large quantities for special needs. For
more information please write to Special Marketing, 201 E. 50th Street, New York,
N.Y. 10022, or call 1-800-800-3246.

Library of Congress Cataloging-in-Publication Data
Salacuse, Jeswald W.
Making global deals : what every executive should know about negotiating abroad /
Jeswald W. Salacuse—1st ed.
p.   cm.
"Originally published in slightly different form by Houghton Mifflin Co. in
1991"—T.p. verso.
Includes bibliographical references and index.
ISBN 0-8129-2090-2 pbk
1. Negotiation in business.   2. International trade.   I. Title.
[HD58.6.S25   1992]   92-9273
658.4—dc20   CIP

Manufactured in the United States of America

9 8 7 6 5 4 3 2

First Paperback Edition

For Donna Booth Salacuse,
in celebration of a very special global deal

Contents

Preface · ix

1 · The Global Deal · 1

2 · Making Deals in Strange Places · 9

3 · Coping with Culture · 42

4 · Ducking Ideologies · 72

5 · Bucking Foreign Bureaucracies · 84

6 · Dealing with Foreign Governments and Laws · 103

7 · Moving Money · 131

8 · Renegotiating Deals · 147

9 · Paddling the Same Canoe · 164

Appendix A · Global Deal Negotiation Checklist · 169

Appendix B · Suggestions for Further Study · 174

Notes · 184

Index · 187

Preface

The world for business has become a kaleidoscope, a place of constantly changing patterns and forms. Established markets vanish in one region as fresh opportunities appear in another. New countries gain independence while others splinter and vanish. Former enemies become allies, and old friends act like adversaries. The forces of international competition shatter the protected markets and special business relationships of company after company.

The kaleidoscope of international events has produced many changes in the last few years. The once monolithic Soviet Union broke up into fifteen autonomous republics, while twelve independent nations in Western Europe formed a single market. As tensions between the United States and Russia evolved into friendship, relations between Japan and America became increasingly tense. The separate economies of the United States, Canada, and Mexico took steps to merge into a North American Free Trade Area. How long these changes will persist is anybody's guess. In the current international system, change is the only constant.

The consequences of these changes have been far reaching for all businesses, large and small. For one thing, they have made meaningless the old, neat distinction between domestic and international business, once so basic in the minds of executives. Indeed, the very term "international business" contains a redundancy, since all business has international connections and implications. For another, they have forced all businesses of any significance to develop a global vision to survive and to become as concerned about their competitiveness abroad as they have traditionally been about their competitiveness at home.

The ability of a business or a country to compete abroad faces many obstacles: protectionism in foreign markets, inadequately trained employees, failures in international cooperation, and lack of knowledge about foreign conditions. While these factors certainly influence global trade and capital flows, discussions about competitiveness often neglect the basic molecule of those flows — the international business deal.

Most commentators take international deal making for granted. They apparently assume that if the right policies and structures are in place, business among nations will automatically follow. Experience clearly shows, however, that negotiating an international business transaction is a difficult, painstaking process that can fail even in the presence of the most favorable policies and institutions. The difference between failure and success often resides in the ability and knowledge of the persons at the negotiating table. If a nation is to become more competitive internationally, a broad segment of its business community needs to be skilled at international deal making. My purpose in this book is to provide business executives, lawyers, and government officials with useful advice on international business negotiation.

I undertook this work out of a long-standing professional interest in how persons from different countries, cultures, ideologies, and political backgrounds join together to undertake common activity. Thirteen years' residence in several countries has allowed me to pursue that interest actively. In both the

United States and abroad, my continuing involvement in international affairs as scholar, professor, adviser, and executive has given me the opportunity to observe at first hand, as well as to participate directly in, negotiations with persons from over thirty countries. Through this book, I hope to share the observations and insights gained from those experiences.

Writing a book is a lot like making a deal in at least one respect—you can't do it alone. I have had generous and indispensable help from many persons in completing *Making Global Deals*. Professor Jeffrey Z. Rubin, my friend, colleague, and partner in many ventures, encouraged this project from the very start, read and commented on the entire manuscript, and provided strong moral support. Donna Booth Salacuse edited the manuscript with her usual skill and exacting standards. I am grateful also to Professor James L. Paddock, Frank Salacuse, and Anne Salacuse for commenting on individual chapters.

In the process of writing the book, I conducted a series of interviews with deal makers whose experience spans the globe. Their insights enriched my writing immeasurably. Deep thanks are therefore owed to Charles F. Adams, Jean Emile Buckens, Albert Cohen, Sidney Feinberg, Robert N. Hornick, Cordell Hull, Arthur Lewis, William F. McSweeny, John H. Morton, Ara Oztemel, Katherine Patterson, Ronald P. Stanton, Eugene Theroux, and Andrei Vandoros. I am also grateful to my colleagues at the Program on Negotiation at Harvard Law School for sharing with me perceptions on the negotiation process in all its dimensions. I was pleased to have the opportunity to develop some of my ideas on international negotiation in articles in the program's publication, *Negotiation Journal*.

Henry Ferris of Houghton Mifflin made many helpful comments on the manuscript and gave genuine encouragement throughout. Katherine Ward was extremely helpful in preparing the bibliography. Thanks are also due to Barney Karpfinger, my agent, who put this particular deal together. And finally, I owe an immense debt of gratitude to Jean Callahan, who supervised the preparation of the many versions of the manuscript while managing the office of the dean of the Fletcher School of Law and Diplomacy with unmatched efficiency and calm. Partial research support for this project was provided by the Center for International Business Education and Research (CIBER) at Tufts University and Bentley College.

MAKING
GLOBAL
DEALS

I

The Global Deal

THE PLAYING FIELD for business is now the globe. National boundaries are no longer business boundaries. Spectacular technological advances, especially in computers and communications, and profound political changes, like those in Europe and the Soviet Union, are causing the "globalization" of business. Companies in all countries are shifting from a national to a worldwide field of action and — especially — of vision.

As a result, businesses large and small must search the entire world for customers and suppliers, for partners and labor, for know-how and finance. IBM enters into a joint venture with Siemens of Germany to do research on semiconductors; Toyota and General Motors build a plant to produce cars in the United States; Daimler-Benz signs a strategic alliance with Mitsubishi to cooperate on everything from autos to aircraft. But the globe is not the playground of giant firms alone. Small businesses, from a three-person packaging company in Atlanta to a family-run toy manufacturer in Seoul, are also active players.

Globalization has placed many new demands on business executives, one of the most important of which is the ability to negotiate deals around the world to get what their companies need. Whether they are from Boise or Beijing, managers have to master what is quickly becoming a basic element of modern business life — the global deal.

For many executives, the move from the domestic to the global deal is not easy. They have had little experience outside their own countries. They speak no foreign language. They have paid scant attention to the constantly shifting relations among nations. Conditioned to see business basically as a domestic activity, managers are often unprepared to conduct international business negotiations with skill and confidence. They frequently approach the task with one of two contradictory, but equally fallacious, attitudes.

For some, international business negotiation is an uncharted sea that is dangerous and mysterious, a place where exotic cultures, foreign languages, unfathomable business practices, and arbitrary bureaucratic traditions make negotiating risky and uncertain. Every deal is different. Experience in China is useless in Saudi Arabia.

Other managers see global deal making merely as an extension of domestic business, an arena in which the skills, attitudes, and knowledge so useful in Akron and Kansas City will work just as well in Accra and Kuala Lumpur. After all, business is business, products are products, and when you come right down to it, international business is really nothing more than making deals in strange places.

Both attitudes are wrong. International deal making is shaped by many common forces, whether negotiations concern a joint venture with a rural commune in China, a Eurodollar loan with a group of London banks, a technology transfer agreement with a Japanese multinational, or a barter arrangement with a Russian trading organization. At the same time, negotiating international business transactions is fundamentally different from making domestic deals.

Books on international negotiation always point to cultural

differences as the principal—often the only—hurdle to be overcome in making deals abroad. So they instruct us on "Negotiating with the Japanese," "Negotiating with the Arabs," and negotiating with countless other people. (You'll even find some of these listed in Appendix B.) Culture is certainly an important factor in making global deals, but it is not the only factor. Many books may tell you how to drink your tea in Osaka or when to cross your legs in Riyadh, but they do not give a general and systematic approach to international negotiations in this new era of global business. *Making Global Deals* seeks to provide you with a general approach that will be equally useful in Saudi Arabia or Japan.

Effective negotiation is not just a matter of following fixed rules and formulas. Every negotiation is special. Each negotiation is affected by a host of different factors in many different ways. The effective deal maker must identify those factors, evaluate them, and then determine a course of action. In many situations, the answer to the question "How should I proceed?" is, quite frankly, "It depends." It depends on the culture; it depends on the political system; it depends on the negotiating environment. In order to develop an appropriate strategy for a particular situation, a negotiator must know the right questions to ask. This book tells you what those questions are, and many of its section headings are in question form to underscore their importance. I hope that through this process, *Making Global Deals* helps you to devise ways to overcome the principal obstacles faced in international business negotiation. Its goal, then, is not formulas, but strategies.

Seven Elements in a Global Deal

This book, a guide to making international business deals, is based on a fundamental principle: all international business negotiations as a group are influenced by seven common factors not ordinarily present in domestic deals. These factors give international business transactions a certain similarity while differentiating them sharply from ordinary domestic business dealings. They also shape the negotiating process powerfully. If you can learn to identify, understand, and deal creatively with these seven factors, you will have taken a big step toward effective global deal making. My purpose is to help you take that step.

Negotiating any deal risks hitting barriers. One side gets locked into a position and refuses to look at other options. The negotiators come to dislike each other and let their personal feelings interfere with the talks. One team thinks the other side is lying. The members of both teams start bickering among themselves.

The skilled negotiator must find ways to deal with these barriers — to get around them, go over or under them, or best of all, to dismantle them entirely. It's a task that needs creativity, sensitivity, and especially patience.

International business negotiators meet these same sorts of obstacles whether they are making a deal to build a timbering joint venture in Indonesia or to arrange an electronics distributorship in Egypt. But international deal makers also face other, special barriers that are not usually found in the ordinary domestic business transaction. The internationally inexperienced manager is usually unprepared to tackle them. These barriers often end up killing a global deal.

To succeed, a negotiator must understand how to cope with

the special *international* negotiating barriers. Overcoming them also requires creativity, sensitivity, and patience. But it demands something more—the ability to recognize these barriers, to understand their structure, and to devise a strategy to attack them.

What are the barriers to a global deal?

The first, and perhaps most obvious, barrier is the *negotiating environment*. The parties are usually located at a great distance from one another. Even in this age of instant global communication and high-speed travel, distance still complicates planning and executing negotiations. One side usually has to travel to the other side's turf to negotiate. For the visitor, that turf is a foreign environment, and that "foreignness" is a potential barrier to deal making.

Culture is a second barrier to making global deals. International business transactions not only cross national boundaries, they also cross cultures. Culture is a powerful factor shaping how people think, communicate, and behave. It also affects their style of negotiation. The cultural differences between a Chinese public-sector plant manager in Shanghai and an American division head of a family company in Cleveland can create a negotiating barrier that in the end will block any deal.

Whether they are Democrats or Republicans, American business executives generally share a common ideology. But in the international arena, business negotiators encounter—and must be prepared to deal with—ideologies vastly different from their own. *Ideology*, then, is the third barrier to negotiating global deals.

The fourth barrier to international business negotiations is *foreign bureaucracy*. Americans are often unprepared for the extensive influence exerted by foreign governments on business activities. Effective international negotiators must know how to deal with a wide variety of foreign organizations, both public and private.

By engaging in international business, a company enters into a world of many different laws and political systems. *Foreign laws and governments* are a fifth barrier to negotiation. An export sale, a direct foreign investment, or a technology transfer brings at least one of the parties to the deal into contact with the laws and government of another country. Not only are these foreign laws and governments largely unknown to visiting global deal makers, but they must also figure out how to cope simultaneously with their own laws and government at home. Failure to overcome this barrier may mean that project income will be taxed by two or more governments, a contract may be governed by two or more legal systems, and a dispute between the parties will be decided by two or more courts— in two or more different ways.

Unlike purely domestic deals, international transactions take place in a world of many currencies and monetary systems. Global deals cross monetary boundaries just as they cross political, cultural, and ideological lines. *Multiple money*, the sixth barrier to a global deal, is always present in negotiation, and it has proved to be insurmountable on numerous occasions.

The seventh and final barrier to global deal making is the risk of *instability and sudden change* so common to the international system itself. Change, of course, is a fact of life, and sudden changes in circumstances are to be found in both domestic and international business. Still, the type and magnitude of change in the international arena appears far greater than in the U.S. domestic setting. The fall of the Shah of Iran, the opening of the Berlin Wall, and the collapse of the Soviet Union are just a few examples of events that had wide and serious consequences for international business deals.

The special barriers, then, for international business negotiators are

1. Negotiating environment
2. Culture
3. Ideology
4. Foreign bureaucracies and organizations
5. Foreign laws and governments
6. Multiple money
7. Instability and sudden change

Any business negotiation, international or domestic, must of course treat a host of commercial issues — price, product quality, size of capital contribution, delivery dates — depending on the nature of the deal being discussed. Conflicts over these issues can become barriers to agreement. In addition to these commercial issues, however, an international business negotiation must deal with the seven special global barriers.

These barriers have a twofold impact on global deal making. First, they increase the risk of failure — the risk that the two sides will not agree, the risk that their agreement will be more apparent than real, the risk that any agreement they make won't stick. Second, these barriers usually lengthen the time it takes to arrive at a deal. As a rule, international deals take longer to conclude than purely domestic transactions of the same variety. McDonald's negotiated for nearly ten years to open its first hamburger restaurant in Moscow, and IBM needed almost two years to secure an agreement to build a computer plant in Mexico. Negotiating a joint venture in China takes an average of two years. As a result, the international business negotiator must have patience and be prepared to commit time that would seem excessive in negotiating a purely domestic transaction in the United States. For Americans raised in the belief that time is money, this aspect of global deal making is often the hardest to master.

Let's now look at each of these barriers to see what they are made of and how a negotiator can climb over, burrow under, and go around them. Better yet, let's discover how negotiators can work together to tear them down.

2

Making Deals in Strange Places

NEGOTIATIONS do not happen in a vacuum. They take place in a specific environment, and the elements of that environment—the place, time, surroundings, events, people—can profoundly influence the course of discussions. In international deal making, the negotiating environment can be a particular barrier, because for one of the parties that environment is distinctly foreign. At its worst, an encounter between a visiting business executive and a foreign environment can produce "culture shock," a phenomenon much discussed by psychologists, which often incapacitates the visitor and may lead a usually dynamic manager to withdraw from contact with other persons, to feel confused, and to become excessively concerned about his health. As a result, he may refuse to eat any local food, no matter how well cooked, avoid meetings with more than two people, and feel compelled to wash his hands every ten minutes.

Even for experienced executives immune to culture shock, negotiating in a strange and unfamiliar environment creates pressures and constraints that, if not dealt with effectively, may slow progress drastically, prevent a good agreement, and worst of all, cause the visiting team to pack its bags and go home without a deal. This chapter examines the more important elements of the negotiating environment to determine how they affect the bargaining process and how negotiators should cope with them. The negotiating environment, like so many other factors in global deal making, confronts an executive with a series of choices and questions. In the search for a deal, as in other pursuits, the first and most basic environmental question is the following.

Your Place or Mine?

The negotiating environment is determined largely by the negotiators' decision on the site for the talks. Site selection is never a casual response to the question "Your place or mine?" In diplomacy, nations often negotiate long and hard about *where* they will meet before they sit down to discuss *what* they will negotiate. The reason for this concern is that the parties almost always assume—and with good reason—that the location they choose will have consequences for the ensuing process and, ultimately, its results. Thus, for both symbolic and functional reasons, George Bush and Mikhail Gorbachev chose to hold their December 1989 summit meeting neither in the United States nor in the Soviet Union—and not even in the territory of any other country. Rather, the two leaders agreed to meet alternately on two ships, the Soviet cruiser *Slava* and the USS *Belknap*, both anchored in the Mediterranean off the coast of Malta.

While few international business executives would go to these extremes to arrange a site for deal making, they should nonetheless consider the impact of site selection on their proposed negotiations and be prepared to adjust to the resulting environment. Generally, parties to a proposed business deal have four options in choosing a site: your place, my place, some other place, or (as a result of advances in international communications) "no place." Let us consider the implications—the advantages and disadvantages—of each of these choices.

MY PLACE

Athletes know that the "home field" or "home court" advantage is often the difference between winning and losing. Similarly, most people probably prefer to hold negotiations on their own territory, rather than on that of the other side. The benefits of negotiating at home are many. First, negotiating on your own territory gives you the advantage of familiarity with the negotiating environment. Your opponents, not you, run the risk of culture shock. They, not you, must deal with unfamiliar foods, strange customs, and a foreign language. You know where everything is located, ranging from telephones and rest rooms to reliable secretarial services and secure areas for private consultation. You need not devote valuable time and energy to getting to know the negotiating environment.

Second, negotiating at home also gives you the possibility of controlling the environment, including the selection and arrangement of the negotiating room, the seating of participants at the negotiating table, and the nature and timing of hospitality and social events. Sometimes a host uses this advantage to create annoyance and pressure on the other side, perhaps by directing visiting negotiators to sit facing a window to be distracted by bright sunlight in their eyes. In a variation on this tactic, one business negotiator used his position as host to gain an advantage by placing his opponents with their *backs* to the window in a high-rise building overlooking Singapore harbor. The negotiation was between an American resident of Singapore and his Malaysian business partner when they had a falling-out in their oil rig servicing business. To protect himself, the American, who had put up most of the capital for the partnership, had seized a valuable boat, the business's only asset, and hidden it under a tarpaulin in the harbor just below the office building. As the negotiations between the hostile partners got under way in the American's office, the tarpaulin was removed and the boat began to leave the harbor. When the American, who was facing the window, saw that the boat had disappeared over the horizon and was therefore safely beyond his partner's reach, he broke off discussions.

Playing host in a negotiation also gives you an opportunity to impress the other team with your organization and to make its members feel indebted to you for your hospitality — factors that may make them more cooperative in the talks. Negotiators have both personal and corporate needs. For a plant manager from the Third World, Eastern Europe, or Russia, a trip to the United States may serve both. While it may lead to a contract for his enterprise, it is also a "perk" that benefits him personally. It should be noted, however, that the effectiveness of your hospitality on the other side may relate directly to the visitors' lack of experience or standing in their organization. Although a trip to the United States may impress a Russian plant manager, it is unlikely to influence a deputy minister.

A host can and often does orchestrate social events to his advantage in other ways. More than one visiting international negotiator has had to labor through the first few negotiating sessions under the debilitating effects of a long airplane trip compounded on arrival by elaborate, late-night entertainment organized by the host. Jet lag is a real problem for the international deal maker. It limits one's ability to concentrate and react quickly and therefore places the visiting negotiator at a disadvantage, as one American deal maker learned on one of his regular trips to Indonesia. When he went to a local bank the morning after his arrival to get a hundred dollars' worth of Indonesian rupiahs, he caused a great commotion by unwittingly writing out and handing the teller a check for $10,000.

Airline magazines offer a lot of advice on handling jet lag, much of which centers around eating special foods in special sequence. No one really knows whether these remedies work. Probably the best way to handle jet lag is to arrive in a country a full day or two before negotiations begin. The extra time gives the body a chance to adjust to the new surroundings. Just as important, it gives the visiting negotiator an opportunity to learn about current conditions in the country, to become better acquainted with his potential partners' business, and to understand the negotiating environment. In the end, the additional cost of an extra couple of days in the country yields dividends in the form of a better deal.

Negotiating at home not only allows you to avoid jet lag, it also gives you easy access to your own experts for needed advice and to superiors in the company for special authorization and consultation. If the other side, during a long-term sales contract negotiation, asks for special financing terms, a negotiation at home allows you to obtain a quick yes or no from your financial vice president. And if the financial department needs persuading, you are in a much better arm-twisting position if you are on the spot than if you have to do it by telephone or fax machine from five thousand miles away.

Finally, negotiating at home is cheaper. Transporting a two-person negotiating team to Tokyo or Seoul and maintaining it in a hotel for a week can easily cost $10,000. Negotiating at home not only saves money, it also saves executive time. Whereas the host negotiator can usually continue to handle the other demands of his job while participating in the negotiation, a visiting U.S. executive in China cannot do the same, despite the marvels of fax and satellite telephone calls. Another disadvantage is that the visiting negotiator is away from his or her personal life—from family, friends, hobbies, and daily routine. The longer one is away, the stronger the emotional drive to conclude the negotiations and return home.

The desire to return home and the costs in time and money of negotiating abroad can put pressure on visiting executives to make a deal (or break off talks) more quickly than they might if they were negotiating in their own country. Sometimes the other side may exploit this situation by deliberately or inadvertently creating delays that run up costs and increase pressures. Many executives have set a date for negotiations with their opposite numbers in a foreign capital only to be told on arrival that a key manager or government official has been called out of the country at the last minute and that the visitors should be patient for a few days until his return. Indeed, these types of delays occur so often that experienced negotiators should take account of them in arranging their travel plans and schedules. One American banker visiting the Cameroons to negotiate a loan failed to take account of this factor in obtaining a visa. He calculated that the negotiation would take a week, so he asked for only a seven-day visa. The negotiation encountered a series of small delays. Because of the importance of the deal and the progress the parties were suddenly making, he decided to stay on until he realized that his visa was set to expire the next day and it would take a week to obtain an extension. He had to make a second trip to the country to close the deal.

While a host may deliberately cause delays to put pressure on the other party, unexpected events can also prolong negotiations. The host may not appreciate the significance of these events to the visitors because he is unaware that the visiting executives are working under inflexible time limits or because, with his cultural background, he attaches less importance to time. For these reasons, experienced negotiators, in arranging a meeting, make very clear to the host the precise date of their departure, even going so far as to specify the exact departure time and number of the flight they will leave on. Some even *understate* the length of time they are prepared to stay in the country. As a general rule, if visiting negotiators, after encountering delays, feel increased pressure to make concessions so that they may return home or go on to other business, it is better to leave as planned and make an agreement with the other side to continue negotiations at another specified time and place.

Sometimes visiting negotiators representing the side with greater power in a deal set a fixed departure date in order to pressure the host to sign a contract. Executives of multinational corporations often use this tactic in their negotiations with small developing countries that are poorly served by international airlines. They arrive Sunday night, hold general discussions on Monday and Tuesday, and present a draft agreement on Wednesday, expressing a strong hope that a contract can be signed by the time their plane leaves on Friday morning. This tactic amounts to an ultimatum, although the source of the ultimatum is made to appear to be the airline rather than the multinational corporation. An ultimatum, although common, is rarely an effective negotiating device. Here, too, rather than make a hasty agreement, it is better for the developing country to defer signing and propose to continue discussions at a later time.

YOUR PLACE

Negotiating on the other side's territory seems to offer only disadvantages: it is costly; the environment is unfamiliar and uncontrollable; lines of communication to the home office are long, uncertain, and insecure. (Will the hotel fax machine operator sell copies of your messages to your home office to the other side?) On the other hand, in most international deals in which you are in the position of a seller, it is only by going to the other side's country that you can bring your product, service, or business needs to that side's attention. The choice of site also has symbolic value. The visiting negotiators are usually those who are the moving force behind the proposed deal. By going to the other side's territory, you show your seriousness of intent and your strong desire to make a deal. This symbolic act may be important in persuading the other side that your company is the one to deal with.

Beyond symbolism, the most important reason of all for negotiating on the other side's territory is *to learn*. An international business negotiation serves many purposes, but one of the most significant, yet unappreciated, is that it gives each side an opportunity to learn about the other, about their businesses, about the conditions in which they must operate. In this respect, comparisons of a negotiation to a sporting event, with allusions to home-field advantage, are false. Executives engaged in making a deal are rarely in the type of competition that ends abruptly when they finish the ninth inning or the fourth quarter. Instead, they are laying the foundation for a continuing relationship, and the successful management of that relationship depends upon how much they know about each other. The need for learning is particularly acute in global deal making, since the parties usually come from much different cultures, political systems, and business orientations. (Indeed, according to recent studies, culture shock itself is not a psychological disorder, but rather the lack of learned skills needed to cope with a new and different environment.)[1] As a result, the effective global deal maker sees the negotiation as an opportunity to learn, and the best way to learn is to visit the other side's territory to conduct the negotiations.

In some cases, negotiating in another country is the only way to get a deal quickly because the other side's negotiators cannot travel easily. Government officials in many developing countries are not permitted to leave their jobs to travel abroad without completing lengthy procedures, and even then they may not be able to secure the necessary hard currency to pay for the trip. So if you want a deal any time soon, you are the one who must get on an airplane. Then there is the problem of the negotiator who has more authority at home than he does abroad. If your opposite number is in that position, it may be better to make the trip yourself. For example, in one negotiation between an American oil company and a Zaire state corporation, President Mobutu insisted on being informed of developments and on making all major decisions. At the end of each day's negotiating session, the Zairian negotiators briefed the president's advisers, who then briefed the president. By the following morning, the chief Zairian negotiator had received his instructions for the day. Ultimately, the two sides signed a contract. Had the negotiations been held in New York instead of Kinshasa, it is doubtful that they would have reached an agreement as quickly as they did.[2]

In global deal making, then, the answer to the question "Your place or mine?" is never automatic. It requires careful study of the particular negotiation in which you are engaged. But as a general rule, one of the best solutions to the site selection question is for the two sides to agree, at the outset of their talks, to alternate the various "rounds" of their negotiation between their two countries, a solution that is particularly appropriate if the negotiations are expected to stretch over a long period of time and the parties contemplate a continuing relationship. For instance, in negotiating a joint venture between a U.S. manufacturer and Egyptian investors to build a dry-cell battery plant in Cairo, the two sides, recognizing that the discussions will require several sessions, might agree to alternate their negotiations between Cairo and New York, or at least that *some* portion of the discussions take place in the United States. Alternating sites allows the Americans and the Egyptians to share the costs and burdens of being host and guest. It also reduces the incentive to take unfair advantage of one's position as host since the other side will have the opportunity to act similarly at the next negotiating session. Most important, moving the negotiations between the two countries assures that both sides will have the opportunity to learn about each other's business and home environment, knowledge that is essential to effective deal making and to building a long-term business relationship.

And even though you are visiting the country, you can still play host by holding the negotiations in a place, like a hotel room, that you select and can control.

SOME OTHER PLACE

The choice of a neutral, third country for negotiation has a certain superficial attraction. Each side gains no special advantage or disadvantage as a result of the location for the talks. At the same time, it has a "worst of both worlds" quality, for it effectively limits the ability of each side to learn much about the other. Whatever inhibits learning inhibits deal making.

Nonetheless, the choice of a third country may be useful if

additional learning is not important to advancing a transaction and if other advantages, such as reduced cost or increased convenience of time, are to be gained. For example, a U.S. manufacturer and a Nigerian distributor, after several negotiating sessions in each other's country, may find it convenient to meet in London to put the finishing touches on the deal. Then, too, if the purpose of the negotiation is to settle a severe business conflict, such as a dispute between joint venturers over the distribution of profits or between a nationalized investor and an expropriating government, a third country may be the best place to hold discussions. In situations of conflict, negotiating in the territory of either party may make the visitors feel they are under pressure or even duress. In the case of a nationalization, both sides may prefer a third country—the investor because it does not want to negotiate in a hostile climate, and the government because it would prefer to reach an agreement with the investor quietly and away from the scrutiny of local media and demands of radical pressure groups at home.

NO PLACE

Rather than choose one site over another, global deal makers can consider the option of avoiding a face-to-face meeting altogether. Instead, whether they are in New York and Tokyo or Los Angeles and London, they can use advanced technology to communicate with one another. Direct-dial international telephone, the fax machine, and video teleconferencing offer low-cost, convenient ways to accomplish global deals. Thanks to satellite communications and fiber optics, businesses all over the world are using these technologies with increasing frequency.

Just as fax was the communications innovation of the 1980s,

video teleconferencing will probably be the innovation of the 1990s. It creates a direct electronic link between two or more negotiating sites and simultaneously broadcasts the images and sounds of each site to the other. Companies are increasingly building their own video teleconferencing rooms, and the services provided by telecommunications companies are becoming cheaper and more available.

While these technologies are important supports for global deal making, they have not yet eliminated the need for face-to-face negotiation in most transactions. Indeed, they may never do so, despite technological advances to make video teleconferencing more lifelike. The principal defect of this technology is that it does not allow sufficient learning and, if relied upon exclusively, compels the parties to negotiate with incomplete information.

An important part of any face-to-face meeting is nonverbal communications—body language, like slight but meaningful gestures and shrugs—and video teleconferencing either conveys such information poorly or not at all. More important, the parties are limited to what they see on the screen. Valuable information about the other side's business environment is not conveyed at all. It can be gained only by a visit to the other party's territory. In addition, video teleconferencing lends a formal air to the talks. It eliminates opportunities for productive socializing—a drink before dinner, a game of tennis at the end of the day, even a simple coffee break—occasions for negotiators to get to know one another better and privately work out problems that may have stymied them at the table.

For these reasons, it would seem that electronic negotiation has the greatest potential in two types of situations: (1) relatively simple transactions, such as the sale of a standard commodity, in which the two sides gain sufficient knowledge through the information exchanged by fax, telephone, or video teleconferencing, and (2) negotiations in which the parties already know each other well. This is one reason that companies with video teleconferencing facilities use them almost exclusively for consultations *within* their organizations rather than for negotiations with outsiders.

Until we have more accurate and more comprehensive communications technologies, global deal making will require a location of some sort. Just as Archimedes, to lift the world, needed a place to stand, global deal makers, to do business, need a place to sit together.

Your Time or Mine?

The negotiating environment is not only affected by place; it is also influenced by time. For the global deal maker, time has several dimensions: local time, home time, and deal time.

LOCAL TIME

In any country, there are good times and bad times to negotiate. Deal making is usually difficult during holidays, vacations, and cultural events that preoccupy or distract persons with whom you are trying to do business. For example, Ramadan, the month when Moslems fast from sunrise until dusk, is generally not the best time to make business deals in the Middle East. In France, August, the traditional month for vacations, is an extremely difficult time to get Parisians to sit at a bargaining table. And most experienced non-Americans have learned that in the United States the weeks between Thanksgiving and New Year's Day are not the best period to gain the full attention of American executives.

Since holidays, national celebrations, and vacations vary

from country to country and from culture to culture, it is important to know the other side's national calendar in planning for negotiations, whether negotiations are to take place on the other side's territory or yours. One of the most frustrating yet all too common experiences is to arrive in a country for negotiations only to find that it is the eve of a four-day national holiday, like the Spring Festival (New Year) in China. Not only are there no negotiations for four days, but a visitor's ability to learn about the country is severely limited because all business and government offices are closed and useful informants are occupied with family and friends. Most of the time, you can avoid this problem by studying the local calendar. But not always. Some countries, particularly in the Third World, have a disconcerting tendency to create surprise holidays, as happened in Zaire. When his wife died, President Mobutu declared a five-day period of national mourning that brought the country to a standstill.

Understanding local time requires more than learning the host country's calendar. Time, or rather the appreciation of the meaning of time, is also affected by local culture. Thus, the significance of a fixed starting time for negotiations may vary from country to country. In Japan, if negotiations are scheduled to begin at 10:00 A.M., Japanese negotiators expect your team to be ready precisely at ten. Failure to arrive on time is viewed negatively. In Nigeria, a ten o'clock starting time is only an approximation. Failure to arrive on time is to be expected. Similarly, whether a negotiation is progressing "too slowly" or whether the response to a proposal has taken "too long" may vary depending on the culture of the negotiator. Americans may interpret the slow pace of discussions as evidence that the other side is dragging its feet and is not seriously interested in making a deal. But a Japanese negotiator, needing to consult many persons within his company each step of the way and intent on building a long-term relationship, considers the pace of the same negotiations as perfectly appropriate. It is therefore important to understand that the other side may have a conception of time different from yours, and you should adjust your negotiating techniques accordingly.

HOME TIME

While negotiations taking place in a particular environment are affected by local conceptions of time, visiting negotiators also remain subject to the daily schedules, annual calendars, and conceptions of time prevailing in their home countries. In effect, they must operate on *both* local *and* home time. American executives who conduct negotiations in Tokyo on local time consult with their New York head office on home time. Because of the difference in time, American negotiators in Japan can call the home office for discussions only after 10:00 P.M. Tokyo time. For negotiations involving Middle Eastern countries — where Friday is a traditional day of rest — and the United States — where offices are closed Saturday and Sunday — the fact that offices of the two countries are functioning simultaneously only four days a week — Monday through Thursday — can affect the progress of discussions. If a document is faxed from New York to Riyadh on Thursday morning, the earliest someone in the U.S. office may expect to see a response from Saudi Arabia is on Monday. Most experienced deal makers handle the problem by arranging to consult with their associates in the United States at their homes after normal working hours. Another technique is to designate a specific person in the home office to "backstop" the deal and to agree on definite times during the day when you will contact each other.

Despite adjustments to local time by American negotiators, the home office remains firmly tied to its usual conceptions of time in judging the progress of any deal. Using home standards, it often challenges its negotiators on the slow pace of the talks. So a visiting executive may feel squeezed between local conceptions of time in which he is negotiating and home conceptions of time to which he must respond as an employee. As a result, a global deal maker may be conducting two sets of negotiations simultaneously—one with the other side to speed up the process, and the other with the home office to convince them that good progress is being made. A Japanese deal maker in the United States often has just the reverse task: to speed up decision making in the Tokyo corporate headquarters while convincing his American counterparts that the talks are making meaningful progress.

Even though negotiations are conducted on your territory, knowing the calendar and conceptions of time of the other side can be useful. It facilitates scheduling negotiating meetings, gives you insight into the time pressures felt by the other side, and enables you to judge the progress of the talks. Although Ramadan may not be a good time to visit certain Islamic countries for negotiations, it may be a very good time to invite negotiators from those countries to come to the United States for discussions. Seeking to avoid fasting rigors enforced by strong social pressures and sometimes by the law, they may readily accept an invitation to go abroad during Ramadan.

Similarly, knowing that a traditional festival is scheduled to take place in a week in the other side's home country may influence your decision to propose new concessions in hopes of securing prompt approval so the visiting team may return home in time to celebrate the holiday with their families.

DEAL TIME

Negotiating an international deal takes longer than negotiating the same kind of deal domestically. As a result, a global deal maker needs patience and must be prepared to commit time to the process.

The negotiation of a deal has its own distinct rhythm. Negotiating a global deal is a process that usually passes through three fundamental phases. In the first, which can be called *Prenegotiation*, the parties determine whether they want to negotiate at all and, if they do, how they will go about it. In the second phase, which might be called *Conceptualization*, the parties try to agree on a common formula or concept for their transaction. The third phase is devoted to working out the *Details* of that formula and precisely how the two sides will carry it out.[3]

Making a global deal is never as neatly segmented as this three-part analysis would suggest. After Prenegotiation, the parties sometimes discuss details before arriving at a formula, instead of agreeing on a formula first. Then, too, the point at which one phase ends and another begins may be difficult to determine with any precision. In some cases, however, the end of one phase may be clearly marked by the preparation of a document. Thus, the Prenegotiation phase may end with a memorandum or agenda setting a time and place for negotiations; the Conceptualization phase may finish with the preparation of a letter of intent or protocol, in which the parties state their intention to negotiate a specific type of transaction such as a joint venture or licensing agreement; and the Details phase concludes with the signing of a final contract.

Each phase has its own rhythm and its own set of problems. Each demands special skill by the negotiators. Prenegotiation (Phase One) consists to a large extent of information gathering

Deal-making Phases

1. PRENEGOTIATION

- Diagnosis
- Information Gathering
- Decision to Negotiate
- Negotiation Agenda

2. CONCEPTUALIZATION

- Definition of Interests
- Proposal and Counterproposal
- Creative Options
- Formula
- Letter of Intent

3. WORKING OUT DETAILS

- Implications of Formula Explored
- Technical Analysis
- Implementation Considered
- Documentation of Agreed Principles
- Contract Concluded

and evaluation. Here, the question is the negotiator's most valuable tool. Conceptualization (Phase Two) consists largely of proposals and counterproposals. Here, creativity of the negotiators comes into play, as they seek to define their interests and to shape a basic concept from which both sides will benefit. In the process, they create and consider a variety of options. The final phase (Details) relies heavily on technical expertise, as the detailed implications of the concept and the problems of its implementation are explored. The parties must then put their agreement in writing in as clear and unambiguous a way as possible.

As negotiations pass from one phase to another, the environment for the talks changes. In Phase One, the general mood is tentative and exploratory. Phase Two, which most deal makers find the most difficult, is marked by great intensity and, in many cases, struggle. Phase Three is characterized by hope for success, but recurring frustration in the face of many minor difficulties often assumes great proportions. The possibility of failure of the talks is present in each phase. A great danger occurs when one party assumes that the talks have progressed from one phase to another when in fact they have not. For example, Americans in negotiations with Japanese sometimes mistakenly believe that they have passed from Prenegotiation to Conceptualization while the Japanese side is really still trying to decide whether it wants to enter serious negotiations toward a common business concept or formula. This type of mistake can lead to suspicions of bad faith, resulting in total failure of the talks. It is therefore important to be certain that you and the other side are at the same phase in the deal-making process. One way of making sure is by using written agendas, letters of intent, and detailed contracts to mark the various stages.

Your Words or Mine?

"The language of international business," one purist has said, "is broken English." Fortunately for American executives, who usually have few linguistic gifts, much of the world's business is conducted in English—an English with a profusion of different accents, cadences, and syntaxes, but a mutually understandable English nonetheless. Language, of course, is crucial to deal making, and it is an important element of the negotiating environment. Because of the widespread use of English in business, the American global deal maker in many instances, but certainly not all, will be negotiating with persons who speak the American's language. Often the American enters this linguistic exchange with the advantage that English is his or her native tongue, while for the other side it is a second or third language.

The degree of fluency in and command of English by the two sides affects the pace and progress of the talks. Therefore, negotiations between an American educated at Harvard Business School and a Nigerian trained at the London School of Economics will ordinarily proceed smoothly from a linguistic point of view. On the other hand, the experienced negotiator knows that English is by no means uniform throughout the globe, and that differences in usage and meaning occur even among the highly educated. As George Bernard Shaw pointed out, England and America are two countries separated by the same language.

Often the other side in a negotiation does not have a strong command of English, a fact that can have a direct effect on the talks. For one thing, it slows the pace of discussions, as each side seeks through repetition and rephrasing to clarify its own and the other side's meaning. In addition, language difficulties can lead to misunderstanding about the nature of the transaction, and they can ultimately create conflict between the two parties. An example of this type occurred in a negotiation between an English construction company and the Sudanese government to build villages for Nubians forced from their traditional homes by the rising Nile waters caused by the construction of the Aswan Dam. When the Sudanese side stated that "time was of the essence in the contract," the English negotiator replied that his company "expected" to meet the deadline. The Sudanese negotiator claimed to have heard him say that the English company "accepted" to meet the deadline. The difference between "expected" (which would merely require the English company to make a good faith effort to finish the work on time) and "accepted" (which legally bound them to do so) may not have sounded like much to the untrained ear, but of course it affected the very nature of the deal. When the company failed to finish the job on the date specified in the contract, a serious conflict arose as to its obligation to pay damages. It was eventually settled only by international arbitration.

The use of linguistic superiority to overwhelm an adversary for whom English is a second or third language rarely works. The wise global deal maker, knowing that future conflict between business partners is *always* costly for *both* sides, seeks to be sure that the other party understands the nature of the deal.

Despite the widespread use of English in international business, American managers occasionally encounter foreign executives who either cannot or will not use English in negotiations. Even if they know the language, they may refuse to negotiate in it because to do so would give the other side a tactical advantage. In this case, an American has only two choices: negotiate in the other side's language, if he or she knows it, or employ an interpreter.

Speaking the other side's language can be extremely useful in building a good relationship with them. But as a general rule you should not negotiate in a foreign language unless you know it extremely well. Otherwise, you will be focusing your attention on the language, rather than on the substance of the deal you are trying to make. Having a translator, even if you know the language, gives you additional time to consider your response to the other side's statements.

Most of the time, parties with different languages employ an interpreter. Linguistic differences and the presence of interpreters change the negotiating environment significantly from that which exists when the two sides speak the same language and can communicate directly. For one thing, the need for an interpreter increases the time required to conduct the negotiation. For another, it raises the risk of misunderstanding between the parties. The linguistic ability of persons calling themselves "professional interpreters" often varies considerably in many countries. Hiring a mediocre professional interpreter can create conflict between the parties that neither may understand. For example, one American company in China was astounded to find that its simple request to bring three typewriters into the country was angrily rejected by government officials on the other side of the table, until it became clear, after an hour of wrangling, that the interpreter had mistranslated the English word "typewriter" as the Chinese word "stenographer."

Even if the interpreter is an expert in the language of the two sides, he or she is rarely also an expert in their two businesses. The context of words is important in giving them meaning, and interpreters are seldom knowledgeable about the relevant business context. The presence of an interpreter increases the number of persons involved in a negotiation and increases its costs. Moreover, instead of coming to know one another directly, the parties have to rely on the interpreter for that knowledge. Depending on his or her degree of skill and integrity, the interpreter can be a clear lens or a murky filter through which information passes easily or is obstructed. But in all cases, the need for an interpreter, at least to some extent, impedes the development of a close working relationship between the two sides. According to one experienced executive, involving an interpreter in a deal is a lot like trying to kiss your girlfriend through a screen door.

There are two types of foreign language interpretation: simultaneous and consecutive. Simultaneous interpretation, frequently found at the United Nations and in diplomatic conferences, is rarely used in international business negotiations because of its great expense and the need for special equipment. Consecutive interpretation, in which a negotiator makes a statement in one language and the interpreter then translates it into another, is by far the more common method. Although the process may seem simple, it complicates deal making and must be managed carefully.

Seven Rules for Using Interpreters

By following a few simple rules, the international business negotiator can make effective use of an interpreter.

1. A negotiation team should hire its own interpreter. Except in cases where special reasons for trust exist, do not rely on the other side's interpreter, unless someone on your team un-

derstands the language and can check the translation. Before hiring an interpreter, try to determine his or her skill and experience from independent, reliable sources.

2. Before negotiations actually begin, hold a briefing meeting with the interpreter to explain the nature of the deal, what you want in the way of translation, and why you want it. For example, if you want a word-for-word translation rather than a summary, make your requirements clear.

3. Guard against interpreters who, because of personal interest or ego, try to take control of the negotiations or slant them in a particular way. This risk may be present if the interpreter also works as a middleman, agent, or business consultant.

4. When negotiating, speak in short, bite-size statements, and pause after each one to give the interpreter a chance to translate your words.

5. Plan each statement carefully so that it is clear, devoid of abbreviations, slang, and business jargon, and delivered slowly. Constantly ask yourself: How can my statements be misunderstood? One inexperienced American executive forgot this rule when he proudly told his Saudi counterparts that he represented a "blue chip company." This drew quizzical looks from both the interpreter and the Saudi executives. The American then launched into a long discussion of the expression "blue chip," only to be told that Saudi Arabia did not allow gambling.

6. Interpretation is difficult and extremely tiring work, so give your interpreter ample opportunity to take periodic breaks.

7. Treat the interpreters, both yours and the other side's, with the respect due professionals. Because the other side's interpreter speaks your language and presumably has insights into your psyche and culture that his employers do not, they may seek his advice about you — whether you are trustworthy,

telling the truth, seem honest. If you have slighted or offended their interpreter in some way during the negotiations, he or she may not give the other side the kind of advice that you would like them to hear. Conversely, if you develop a friendly relationship with the interpreter, he or she may provide you with much useful information about the other side, as one Japanese interpreter did when he let it slip that the head of his delegation believed he would lose face if he returned to Tokyo without a contract.

A final linguistic decision is to determine the language of the contract. An American company normally wants English alone to be the language of its agreement, but the other side may push just as hard to have the contract written in its own language. A compromise is to have both an English- and foreign-language version of the contract and to provide that both versions are equally authoritative. Unless the translations are done extremely skillfully, the parties may later find differences in the two versions that require further negotiations to settle.

Your Team or Mine?

The negotiators themselves form part of a negotiating environment. Wrong people at the table can kill a deal, no matter how good it looks. Skilled and prepared negotiators, on the other hand, can turn a bad situation around. It is therefore important to select and prepare the negotiating team with care. For help in preparation, executives should consult Appendix A, the Global Deal Negotiation Checklist.

The size and expertise of the negotiating team will depend on the nature of the deal and the parties' cultural backgrounds. One or two people with knowledge of sales can negotiate a long-term supply contract. Negotiating a manufacturing joint venture requires a larger team and a broader range of expertise. Some business cultures, like the Chinese, tend to put together large negotiating teams, while others, like the Americans, prefer small ones. In some cultures, the use of lawyers as negotiators raises concerns on the other side about possible future lawsuits. In those cases, it may be better to keep the lawyer in the background or to refer to him as an "adviser" or "counselor" rather than a "lawyer," a person whose primary role in many countries is to litigate disputes.

The team should agree on a single spokesperson. Effectiveness of a negotiating team can be severely diminished when more than one person speaks on its behalf. Several voices give several different messages, a situation that confuses the other side and ultimately leads it to question your side's credibility. While a team usually consists of specialists and technicians, the team leader should be a generalist with a broad vision, a person who can integrate the various technical requirements into a broad concept or formula that will be the basis for the deal. In one negotiation between an American construction company and a Turkish public-sector corporation, both teams consisted only of specialists. Neither had a generalist. As a result, the technicians on each side argued about technical points. No one was capable of developing a general framework for the deal, so the talks ended after a week of fruitless bickering.

The team should prepare for the negotiation before it leaves home. A team is inviting disaster if its prevailing attitude is merely one of "Let's go to Beijing and hear what the Chinese have to say about making a deal with us." Instead, the team should conduct extensive preparatory meetings during which members share what they know about the other side, determine the information they need to get, anticipate the other side's proposals and positions, identify their own and the other side's underlying interests, and, most important, decide on a "bottom line," the point at which they will walk away from the discussions.[4] They should make that decision before they begin negotiations rather than after the bargaining has begun. Otherwise the heat of negotiations may cause them to make concessions they will later regret. As part of preparation, the team should engage in simulated negotiations and role-play to anticipate the negotiating situations they expect to meet.

The team should allocate specific functions and tasks among its members. To smooth the negotiations, specific team members should be given definite tasks related to the deal-making process, including note taking, transportation arrangements, logistics, communicating with the home office, and arranging for an interpreter.

The team should prepare the necessary documents for the deal in advance. One of the most useful ways to get ready for negotiations is to prepare a draft of the agreement you hope to make. That brings us to a final question in thinking about the negotiating environment.

Your Draft or Mine?

For many persons, the word "negotiation" evokes images of a process that goes through a fixed sequence of phases: the parties first state their positions and interests, then make concessions and adjustments, eventually reach an understanding if all goes well, and finally write their agreement on paper. According to this view, the parties talk first and write last.

In many negotiations, however, the sequence of events is just the reverse. A common opening gambit in negotiations is for one party to present the other with a detailed document, known variously as a draft, model, prototype, or standard-form agreement, to serve as a basis for discussions. Thus, in practice, negotiators often write first and then talk.

The presentation of a comprehensive draft agreement as a first step is a frequent practice in both business and diplomatic negotiations. Multinational corporations use draft contracts to sell jet aircraft, form joint ventures, and lend Eurodollars. Governments seeking bilateral relationships of varying sorts with foreign countries often launch negotiations by asking the other side to comment on a draft treaty.

PURPOSES OF THE DRAFT

A draft or model agreement serves many purposes for the side presenting it. First, its preparation is an opportunity for negotiators representing an organization to consult with important internal and external constituencies and to decide on an acceptable negotiating position. This preliminary consultation is not only important preparation for the negotiations themselves, but it also gives the negotiators some assurance that any deal that closely follows the draft will be approved by the home office. Second, since the government or corporation often contemplates negotiating similar arrangements with many different parties, the model or draft agreement is an efficient means of informing potential negotiating partners about the type of contract or treaty that the proposing party favors. Uniformity of contract language simplifies administration of numerous agreements. It can also avoid later charges of discrimination and resulting demands for renegotiation by countries or corporations believing that others have received better treatment than they have. Beginning all negotiations with the same basic draft is generally seen as a cost-effective, efficient practice.

But perhaps the main reason for submitting a draft agreement at the beginning of negotiations is that it gives the proposing party a tactical advantage. Many experienced negotiators believe that "the one who controls the draft controls the negotiations." If the other side accepts the draft as the basis for discussions, the presenter has in effect set the agenda of the negotiation and, more important, established the conceptual framework for negotiating the deal. To a large extent, the party submitting the draft fixes the terms of reference, while the other side (at least at the outset) is merely reacting to the draft's language rather than advancing specific proposals of its own. Indeed, the party that receives the draft may become so preoccupied with the text that it neglects its own negotiating objectives and interests.

RISKS OF THE DRAFT

Although controlling the draft may allow you to control the negotiation, wise negotiators should be careful about applying this bit of conventional wisdom indiscriminately. Insistence on your own draft may enable you to dominate the negotiation at the outset, but it may also obstruct an agreement in the long run. Scholars of negotiation theory urge negotiators to focus on interests, not positions, to search for creative options for mutual gain, and to find a "formula" to accommodate competing goals.[5]

Insisting on one's own draft in a negotiation may frustrate this useful advice. For one thing, putting a draft on the table at an early stage in the negotiations may lock the parties into bargaining positions, thereby obstructing a search for common interests and creative formulas. A draft or model agreement is, after all, nothing more than a detailed statement of a position. Then, too, if one of the functions of the early phase of a negotiation is to allow both sides to gather and share as much information as possible about one another, focusing at the outset on the draft is likely to hamper this vital process.

Although corporations may believe that their model contracts have universal application, they may in fact be inapplicable to particular local conditions or a specific situation under discussion; consequently, unyielding insistence on their terms may sometimes lead to results that are unsatisfactory for both sides. For example, the refusal by an American fast food company to change its master contract language contributed to a business failure in Australia. The final contract retained the franchiser's standard provision requiring the construction of top-quality, snowproof buildings. Since Melbourne is not subject to heavy snowfalls, the resulting construction costs to the franchisee placed an unnecessary and, ultimately, a fatal burden on the Australian operation.

Finally, since the party introducing a draft is usually in a superior bargaining position, the other side may view the presentation of the draft as an act of arrogance and a not-too-subtle signal of an unequal relationship between the parties. Consequently, placing a detailed draft on the table at the very beginning of a negotiation may instill suspicion and hostility in the other side, factors that, at the very least, will slow reaching an agreement.

All the above suggests that negotiators should not automatically introduce a prepared draft as an opening gambit in all negotiations. Instead, they should carefully analyze each situation to determine the appropriate time to present their draft in the negotiation process, if at all. They should also recognize that an inflexible insistence on the draft's terms is likely to prolong negotiations, and may even derail any chance of agreement.

COPING WITH THE OTHER SIDE'S DRAFT

Suppose the other side puts its draft on the table at the start of discussions. What can you do about it? Three approaches suggest themselves.

1. Prepare a Counterdraft

The obvious approach is to counter the proposed draft with a draft of your own. The counterdraft may be one specifically prepared for the negotiation in question or one drawn from a completed agreement in another transaction.

Introducing a counterdraft is an effort to share control of the negotiations and to create an alternate conceptual framework. The preparation of a counterdraft also has the benefit of forcing you to think through your interests and to develop your own position on the issues under discussion. In addition, a party who objects strongly to the original draft may feel that submission of a counterdraft is a positive, constructive way of making its concerns known to the other side.

Although the counterdraft tactic may seem obvious, negotiators often fail to use it. Preparation of a counterdraft, especially on highly technical matters, requires a level of expertise that a party simply may not have. Developing countries negotiating with multinational corporations often find themselves in this position. The preparation of a counterdraft without adequate knowledge of the subject could result in a text that puts the developing country at a greater negotiating disadvantage than if it had chosen to base discussion on the original draft prepared by the multinational firm. Even if a country has the expertise, it may not be in a position to devote sufficient personnel and time to preparing a counterdraft for a single transaction, in contrast to a multinational corporation that can afford to assign a team of experts for an extended period of time to produce a form contract.

Countering one draft with another may introduce an added element of disharmony into negotiations, and a party in a weak position may therefore hesitate to adopt this approach. The introduction of a counterdraft almost always results in a "duel of drafts," with each side insisting that *its* text be made the basis for discussion. The side offering the first draft invariably argues that any changes will make subsequent ratification by the home office uncertain, if not impossible, since all necessary departments have approved it. The party submitting the counterdraft can make the same argument to support its own text. How can a potential stalemate be avoided?

One solution may be for the negotiators to accept both drafts for discussion and to work together to present a single text. This process involves the parties in preparing one document that incorporates common principles emerging from the two texts and their discussions. To accomplish this task, the parties have to look beyond stated positions in order to determine underlying interests and develop creative, mutually satisfactory solutions. The use of a computer spread sheet that sets out side by side the pertinent provisions of the two drafts can facilitate the task of preparing a single text.

2. Discuss Principles First

When confronted with a draft early in a negotiation, you may counter it by politely requesting the other side to put it aside temporarily while the two of you discuss basic principles and concepts to govern your relationship. You might, in a joint venture negotiation, rather than discuss provisions of a draft agreement article by article, first outline the major elements of your venture, like allocation of risk, distribution of profits, duration, and control. As you reach agreement on each major issue, write your general understanding in the form of simple statements. These then become the framework for the details of your contract, replacing the first draft originally proposed by the other side.

3. Use the Draft but Not Its Order

In many circumstances, you may have no choice but to accept the other side's draft as the basis for negotiation. They may simply have too much bargaining power, or you may have few other options. In such situations, you should not simply discuss the draft provision by provision, beginning with the first article and proceeding in order to the last. Rather, you should determine the principal issues to be discussed and present them for consideration in the order you judge appropriate. This approach, at the very least, enables you to shape the order of the agenda and perhaps avoid being locked into the conceptual framework that the other side seeks to impose through its draft.

For the inexperienced global deal maker, the physical elements of the negotiating environment are often the most startling and the most difficult to cope with at first. Strange places, foods, languages, and surroundings seem to be insurmountable barriers to doing business. In reality, with proper study and planning, the problems of the negotiating environment can be easily understood and dealt with. What is much harder to understand and to relate to is what is inside of the other team's heads. Let's now turn to two of those elements — culture and ideology.

3

Coping with Culture

NEGOTIATING is communicating. Effective negotiation is above all good communication. Poor communication, on the other hand, kills deals.

Words Alone Are Not Enough

Negotiators do not live by words alone. Like anybody else, they communicate with both words *and* actions. In fact, most important emotional messages at a negotiating table — like those conveying friendship or anger, confidence or mistrust — are expressed nonverbally by gestures, tone of voice, or facial expressions. When the other side says "Of course" in response to your simple statement of fact, those two words can mean anything from "That's a good point" to "I understand" to "Any idiot knows that! How stupid do you think I am?" Only the speaker's actions and voice make clear which meaning is intended. The opposition's interpretation of your original statement as helpful advice or a condescending put-down may have depended on your own tone of voice and body language at the time you spoke.

The Negotiator's Three Cameras

To communicate effectively, skilled negotiators must constantly and simultaneously be aware of three things throughout a negotiation: their own words and actions; the meaning that the other side gives to those words and actions; and the words and actions of the other side.

As a result, a good negotiator is like a director in a television studio watching three TV monitors showing the images taken by three different cameras of the same set. Each monitor displays a different angle or dimension of the same activity. Like the television director, a negotiator must constantly process information from each of the monitors, then make decisions about next steps. The global deal maker faces a particular challenge because the information conveyed by those cameras cannot be understood fully without a knowledge of the other side's culture, ideology, and political system.

For most of us, our ways of speaking and acting are habits, automatic responses used in our dealings with other people. It is dangerous, however, to take those habits unthinkingly to a negotiating table. For example, referring to someone by first name after an introduction may be second nature to you in a social setting, but the other side in a negotiation may find it offensive at a first meeting. You therefore need to consider carefully possible consequences of statements and actions *before* actually using them to communicate, just as a television director studies a monitor before deciding to transmit an image on the airwaves. Therefore, camera number one for a negotiator should focus constantly on his or her own contemplated words, actions, and gestures.

The meaning that we intend and the meaning that the other

side gives to our words and actions can be two very different things. When one side says, "We expect to deliver by September 1," they intend a good faith effort to ship goods by that date but are not making any legally binding commitment to do so. The other side, however, may interpret that statement as a firm obligation to deliver. Because the risk of misunderstandings in communications between human beings is always present in any transaction, camera number two should be constantly focused on how the other side is reacting to you, and particularly on whether they have understood a statement in exactly the way you intended it. One way of operating camera two is to imagine yourself in the place of the other side.

Finally, camera number three scrutinizes the statements and actions of the persons across the table. It seeks to understand their meaning and intent. Sometimes camera three gives you only enough information to develop a further line of questions to find out what they intend. When the other side says they "expect to deliver," are they making a commitment? What was the meaning of their prolonged silence after your previous comment? Does that quizzical look on their faces mean that they doubt your sincerity, or is it just that the interpreter has botched the translation? These are the images that negotiators rely on camera three to pick up.

The three imaginary cameras and monitors are essential equipment to bring to the negotiating table. The failure to use all three constantly and simultaneously throughout a negotiation can lead to failures in communication and ultimately in the talks themselves.

The Great Cultural Divide

The risk of communication failure is always present in any negotiation, domestic or international. Although two American executives share a common language, culture, ideology, and business philosophy, their negotiations can easily fail as a result of misunderstanding each other's words and actions. When two negotiators come from *different* cultures, say, from the United States and Japan, the risks of misunderstanding during a negotiation increase exponentially. Differences in culture divide business executives from different countries. Culture is a special barrier in international deal making. This chapter first discusses how culture affects negotiations and then suggests ways that the global deal maker may cope with culture.

What do we mean by culture? Culture includes the socially transmitted beliefs, behavior patterns, values, and norms of a given community. It consists of rules, concepts, categories, and assumptions that the people of that community use to interpret their surroundings and guide their interactions with other persons within the society. Two Americans who negotiate a business deal bring to the table the values, beliefs, and background information of American culture, and they use the elements of that culture subconsciously to interpret each other's statements and actions. So when a California film producer and a New York agent for a movie star agree to "do lunch and talk contract," they both know that they will be discussing a detailed document covering not only salary, but billing, advertising, rehearsal time, dressing room, facilities, and a host of other matters peculiar to the U.S. entertainment industry. If, after their first martini, the agent says, "We want a gross deal," the producer understands immediately that the film star is seeking a portion of the film's gross revenues before the deduction of expenses. And when the producer replies, "Nicholson he's not!" the agent knows that he has to convince the producer that his client is indeed in the category of performers who, like Jack Nicholson, have reputations that command a percentage of gross revenues.

Without adequate background knowledge, a person from another country—perhaps a bilingual Russian bureaucrat or an Argentinean rancher with excellent English—would find it difficult to understand the exchange between the producer and the agent because their words alone—like "Nicholson," "gross deal," and even "contract"—have meaning only when interpreted in the light of American culture and the U.S. entertainment business. In most cases, words are just a code that you cannot understand unless you understand the context and the background.

When persons from two different cultures meet for the first time, they generally do not share a common pool of information and assumptions to interpret each other's statements, actions, and intentions. In short, they do not know the code. As a result, difficulties in communication can easily arise between them, and these difficulties may greatly complicate the negotiating process in several ways. For one thing, it may cause them to misunderstand each other's statements.

Read My Lips

If one American executive responds to another American's proposal by saying, "That's difficult," the response, interpreted against American culture and business practice, probably means that the door is still open for further discussion, that perhaps the other side should sweeten its offer. In any event, the fact that the proposal is "difficult" is not taken to mean that it is impossible. Coming from a "can-do" culture, the American presses the proposal, perhaps changing it somewhat in hopes of gaining acceptance. In some other cultures, particularly those in Asia, persons are reluctant to say a direct and emphatic no, even when they mean it. So when a Japanese negotiator, in response to a proposal, says, "That is difficult," he is clearly indicating that the proposal is unacceptable. "It is difficult" means "no" to the Japanese, but to the American it means "maybe." American persistence in pressing a proposal in this situation would be viewed by the Japanese as overly aggressive and even hostile behavior.

Watch My Moves

Cultural differences create difficulties not only in understanding words, but also in interpreting actions. For example, while Americans and Canadians may find it perfectly appropriate to conduct business discussions at lunch, Mexican and Brazilian executives may consider serious business negotiations totally out of place in that setting. Thus, there is a sharp cultural difference as to when and where negotiation is or is not proper.

Culture also influences the conduct of executives at the negotiating table. Most Westerners expect a prompt answer when they make a statement or ask a question. Japanese, on the other hand, tend to take longer to respond. As a result, negotiations with Japanese are sometimes punctuated with periods of silence that seem excruciating to an American. For the Japanese, the period of silence is normal, an appropriate time to reflect on what is said. The fact that they are not speaking in their native language lengthens even more the time needed to respond.

From their own cultural perspective, Americans may interpret Japanese silence as rudeness, lack of understanding, or a cunning tactic to get the Americans to reveal themselves. Americans can become even more agitated when they observe certain members of the Japanese negotiating team sitting on the other side of the table with their eyes closed. Rather than wait for a response, the American tendency is to fill the void with more words by asking additional questions, offering further explanations, or merely repeating what they have already said. This response to silence may confuse the Japanese, who are made to feel they are being bombarded by questions and proposals without being given adequate opportunity to respond to any of them.

On the other hand, Latin Americans, who place a high value on verbal agility, have a tendency to respond quickly. Indeed, they may answer a point once they have understood it even though the other side has not finished speaking. While inexperienced American executives are sometimes annoyed by Japanese delays in responding, they become equally agitated in negotiations with Brazilians by what Americans consider to be constant interruption.

Cultural patterns may also influence the setting for international deal making in other ways. Westerners expect business negotiations to be conducted in private, that the other side will devote exclusive attention to the proceedings, and that interruptions will be few. In many parts of the Arab world, these expectations may not be fulfilled. It is common for negotiations in business or government offices in Egypt or Saudi Arabia to be interrupted frequently by telephone calls, secretaries wanting signatures, and even visitors seeking an important word with the Arab official or businessperson. While Western executives may interpret these interruptions as a sign of discourtesy or lack of interest by their Arab host, the Arab, sensitive to the intricate web of personal relations that bind him to his society, feels that it would be extremely rude to refuse a telephone call or visit from a friend or associate. Surely the visiting Western negotiators cannot mind an interruption of just a few minutes.

Like images on a television screen, a silent Japanese with his eyes closed or an Arab constantly bounding up from a table to embrace a guest has no specific meaning until it is interpreted within a definite cultural and situational context. Watching those images, an American who is told that both the Arab and the Japanese are involved in a business negotiation would conclude, by applying his own cultural assumptions, that neither is particularly interested in the negotiations and that no deal is likely to result. Similarly, an Arab viewing the Japanese's apparently sleepy behavior, and the Japanese seeing the Arab's somewhat frantic activity, would probably come to the same conclusion, since their own cultural background would also lead them to believe that the foreign executive or official they were watching lacked interest in the discussions.

But when viewing his own countryman on the television screen and interpreting his actions through his own culture, an Arab observer would conclude that the Arab executive's behavior was perfectly appropriate to serious deal making and a Japanese observer would most assuredly reach the same verdict about his own countryman. The reason for this difference in results is not national bias but that culture gives meaning to words and actions. In watching their own countrymen, they have the knowledge to arrive at the intended meaning; when they watch a foreigner they do not. Similarly, U.S. executives negotiating an international transaction will not be able to interpret the images on their three imaginary television monitor screens correctly unless they know the culture of the persons with whom they are trying to make a deal. Without that knowledge, American executives abroad have difficulty in determining whether their own words and actions are appropriate (camera one), whether the other side has understood them as the Americans intended (camera two), and whether they have correctly evaluated the meaning of the other side's statements and behavior (camera three). Lacking that knowledge, American executives have a tendency to evaluate those images in terms of their own culture and background, an approach that almost invariably leads to misunderstanding, conflict, and ultimately, failure.

Learn My Ways

In addition to complicating communications and the negotiating process, cultural differences also influence the form and substance of the deal you are trying to put together. Elements of the transaction itself may have to be shaped to fit cultural values and expectations. For example, in many parts of the Moslem world, where Islamic law prohibits the taking of interest on loans, you may need to restructure or relabel finance charges in a deal as ''administrative fees'' in order to gain acceptance at the negotiating table.

More substantively, products have to be adapted to foreign markets; management systems need to be adjusted to local conditions; and labor practices must be changed to meet foreign workers' cultural patterns. A U.S. software manufacturer learned this lesson in Japan when it introduced a personal computer program that had been highly successful in the United States. The company recognized at the outset that the program would have to be translated into Japanese. But as development studies progressed, it learned that other, more subtle changes would also have to be made. For one, the program emitted a beeping sound each time the operator made a mistake, a standard feature in use in the United States. Japanese work closer together than Americans do. They are not divided by partitions or located in separate offices. They also have a heightened concern about loss of face. In that environment, a beep not only made it clear to the personal computer operator that a mistake had been made, but it also announced that fact to coworkers, thus causing the operator acute embarrassment. To assure acceptance of the software program in Japan, the manufacturer dropped the beeping signal for most computer errors.

While many specific cultural adjustments to products and systems cannot be foreseen at the time a deal is negotiated, wise executives take account of the need for this kind of adaptation in structuring their transactions. Therefore, they seek to avoid strict deadlines in the development of foreign manufacturing facilities, recognizing that local culture may require time-consuming adjustments to production systems. Changes can also be costly; consequently, a deal should also specify who will pay for those adjustment costs.

This brief overview makes it clear that culture has a multifaceted impact on deal making. It influences communication, negotiating behavior, the structure of a deal, and the actual operation of the resulting business. A skilled negotiator should always be alert to the effect of culture on deal making at each step of the process so as to avoid making unnecessary mistakes.

Dealing with Another Culture

Once you realize how culture may affect negotiations, you must prepare yourself to deal with it. As you seek to approach the culture in a particular country, you need to answer a fundamental question:

WHOSE CULTURE IS IT ANYWAY?

A culture comes from a particular group or community. The world is filled with an enormous number of distinct cultural groups. Each group has its own set of traditions and beliefs — traditions and beliefs that in theory, at least, affect the thinking and negotiating styles of executives and government officials who are members of that group and whom you may meet at the negotiating table.

A skilled negotiator tries to know as much as possible about the other side. The first task you face in an international deal is to identify the cultural group to which your counterpart belongs and then to learn something about that culture. In undertaking this exercise, inexperienced executives should avoid lumping vaguely related cultures together in the same general grouping. For instance, one occasionally hears references to "Asian culture" and "Asian negotiating styles," and to "African culture" and "African negotiating techniques." These kinds of categorizations are oversimplifications. While the peoples of Asia share certain cultural traits, one can hardly call them a single cultural group. The culture of Japan is different from that of Korea, and the negotiating style of most Japanese is certainly distinct from that of most Koreans. Africa also has great diversity in cultures and negotiating styles.

A specific cultural group may coincide with a particular nationality. The French, the Germans, and the Japanese each have more or less homogeneous cultures. But culture and nationality are not always the same. Within Nigeria, for example, the culture of the Ibos in the largely Christian south and the Hausas in the mainly Moslem north are different and so are the respective deal-making and business styles of these two tribal groups. Individual countries may have several distinct cultural groups, each with its own values and beliefs, its special relationships to its government, and its history of conflicts with others. An understanding of these cultural distinctions within a country can influence the communication between parties, the process of deal making, the structure of a transaction, and even the decision of whether to negotiate at all.

Belonging to a particular cultural group has political as well as social consequences. For this reason, it may be important to know whether you are negotiating with a Hindu or a Moslem in India, with a native *prebumi* or an ethnic Chinese in Indonesia, with a Moslem or a Copt in Egypt, or with a Kongo or a Muluba in Zaire. If you are negotiating a joint-venture deal with a member of a cultural minority that is out of favor with its government, you may have difficulty securing government approvals needed to launch a project. It is better to understand this risk at the outset of negotiations rather than to realize it after you have invested money and time in making the deal. On the other hand, the fact that the other team includes a member of a cultural or tribal minority may lead to internal disagreements that give you opportunities to strike a deal that a completely united team would never let you get away with.

Learning Another Culture

How do you come to know the other side's culture? Ideally, learning a culture other than your own requires several years' study, mastery of the local language, and prolonged residence in the country of that culture. An American faced with the job of negotiating a strategic alliance with a Turkish company in Ankara in two weeks' time cannot, of course, master Turkish culture that fast. At best, an executive can learn only enough to cope with some of the principal effects that Turkish culture may have on making the deal.

History is an important window on a country's culture. So at the very least, the executive should read a history of modern Turkey. If time permits, he or she might consult anthropological studies, reports on the current political situation, and accounts, if any, on "Negotiating with the Turks."

Consultation with persons who have had significant business experience in Turkey can also be helpful. Banks with strong financial links to Turkey and corporations with subsidiaries or long-established relations in the country can also be excellent sources of advice on coping with Turkish culture. The U.S. Department of State in Washington, particularly through its Turkey desk, and the American embassy or consulate in Turkey, particularly through its commercial officers, may also be able to give you good advice on negotiating business deals in that country. American companies often ask the embassy's advice about the political situation or general business conditions in the country, but sometimes forget to ask about the negotiating experiences of other American companies with local public- and private-sector corporations. Another source of advice on Turkish culture may be a nearby American university with a Middle East studies center or Turkish program. While academic institutions can certainly provide much valuable information, you must be able to give them fairly specific guidance on the kind of advice you are seeking. A general request for information on Turkish culture is liable to elicit information that is too theoretical or too general to be of direct use to the practical negotiator.

Finally, if you have hired a Turkish lawyer, business consultant, or interpreter to work on the deal with you, these individuals can offer much valuable advice on how Turkish culture may affect the negotiating process, communications between the parties, the structure of the transaction, and the execution of the deal itself. Note, however, that often these professionals, hired to do a specific job, are reluctant to give advice on matters outside their assigned domains unless you specifically seek their views. You should encourage them to counsel you on matters relating to culture, politics, and the general process of interaction with the other side.

RUNNING TRUE TO FORM

If rule number one in international negotiations is "know the culture of the other side," rule number two is "avoid over-reliance on that knowledge." Not all Japanese evade giving a direct negative answer. Not all Arabs allow interruptions during negotiations. Not all Mexicans object to discussing business at lunch. Not all Germans tell you specifically what they think of a proposal. In short, the negotiator who enters a foreign culture should be careful not to allow cultural stereotypes to determine his or her relations with local businesspersons.

Just as American minorities and women take offense at being labeled by certain traits or characteristics, foreign business executives also take offense if they feel you are not treating them as individuals, but as members of a particular cultural or ethnic group. To tell a Brazilian executive with whom you are dealing that you expect him to be late for meetings because he is "Latin" does little to develop an effective working relationship. To make a joke with your potential Dutch partner about his country's reputation for being tight is hardly a constructive way to begin discussions about cost sharing. Even if you do detect certain cultural traits in the negotiating approach of the other side, and if, indeed, they are running true to form, it is never wise to mention it.

In addition to giving offense, cultural stereotypes can be misleading. Many times the other side simply does not run true to the negotiating form suggested by books, articles, and consultants. The reason, of course, is that forces besides culture may influence a person's negotiating behavior. Specifically, these forces include the negotiator's personality, the organization he or she represents, and the context of the particular negotiation in question. Culture has a role in each of these three, but other factors are at work as well. Let us look briefly at each of them.

PERSONALITY

None of us is a cultural robot. While culture certainly influences personality, numerous other factors affect it as well: biology, education, experience, and relationships with family, friends, and colleagues, to name just a few. The same is true with negotiators from other countries. A Western businessperson who meets highly skilled negotiators from other countries, such as former oil minister Sheik Zaki Yamani of Saudi Arabia or Sony chairman Akio Morita of Japan, may be tempted to conclude that because of their sophistication, they are somehow less attached to their own culture or that they have become "Westernized." Such conclusions are not only culturally arrogant, they are also greatly deceptive. Yamani remains thoroughly Saudi and Morita is still very Japanese. What both have gained through years of experience in international business is the knowledge of how to communicate with persons from other cultures. To the Western businessperson, Yamani and Morita seem "Westernized" because they are communicating with Westerners in a way Westerners readily understand. Thus a Japanese executive with an M.B.A.

from Stanford and several years' experience in global business may respond to an American proposal with a firm and clear no (although he might never do so at home) because he knows how to communicate with American executives in a language they understand.

What all of this suggests is that in approaching an international negotiation, you should try to learn as much as possible about your counterpart as a *person*, not just as a representative of a particular culture. Although the research tools and sources upon which we rely for this kind of information may not be as readily available in foreign countries as they are in the United States, useful information may be obtained from newspapers, banks, and U.S. embassies. In small countries, where the educated class is few in numbers, background information may be gained simply by talking to people.

ORGANIZATION

The behavior of a negotiator can also be affected by the organization he or she represents. An ordinarily passive Indonesian executive may become quite aggressive in a negotiation because his superiors have made it clear that a sought-after promotion depends on his making an advantageous deal in this particular negotiation. Similarly, a usually amiable Mexican bureaucrat may become strident and rigid in discussions with American executives on instruction from the minister in charge of his department.

Understanding the structure and dynamics of the other side's organization is indispensable to deal making. In one negotiation between a Korean and an American company, a junior member of the Korean team inadvertently blurted out over drinks that his boss felt extreme pressure to take a signed contract back to Seoul. With that information, the Americans held firm to their position and concluded a favorable deal. Chapter 5 examines the influence of foreign governmental and business organizations on making global deals.

CONTEXT

The context of a particular negotiation in which executives are engaged can affect the negotiating behavior of one or both sides. How two executives relate to each other—whether they like or trust each other—can influence the negotiation as profoundly as their individual cultural characteristics. Similarly, whether they are working under externally imposed deadlines, such as a bank credit commitment that is about to expire, can influence the pace of negotiations as much as culture.

Ten Ways Culture Affects Negotiations

While warning against cultural stereotypes and oversimplifications, all experienced negotiators acknowledge that cultural differences between negotiators are an important and special factor in global deal making. A knowledge of the other side's culture allows a negotiator to communicate, to understand, to plan, and to anticipate more effectively. The enormous number and great diversity of the world's cultures make it impossible for any negotiator, no matter how skilled and experienced, to understand fully the culture that he or she encounters. How, then, should an executive entering international negotiations prepare to cope with cultures in making global deals? One approach is to try to identify the specific ways in which cultural traits affect the negotiating process.

While culture can influence a business deal in many ways, as noted above, it generally has a direct impact on the deal-making process itself in only ten substantial ways.[1] A knowledge of these ten factors allows you to analyze the negotiator you are facing and enables you to develop an effective way of communicating with your counterpart. It is also useful to measure your own negotiating style against these ten factors to see how you appear as a negotiator to executives from other countries. Each factor represents a continuum along which negotiating behavior may be placed between two identified poles.

Some may argue that these traits are a result of personality rather than culture. Culture certainly does not determine behavior, but it does predispose persons of a given cultural group to act in certain ways in specific situations. But rather than pursue this debate, it is enough to point out that these ten traits are common in negotiating behavior and, whether they are caused by personality or culture or both, the practical negotiator must learn to deal with them.

1. Negotiating Goal: Contract or Relationship?

An initial question is whether the two sides in a negotiation have the same goal and see the deal-making process in the same light. It is possible for businesspersons from different cultures to interpret the very purpose of their negotiation differently. For many Americans, the purpose of a business negotiation, first and foremost, is to arrive at a signed contract between the parties. Americans view a signed contract as a definitive set of rights and duties that strictly binds the two sides, an attitude succinctly summed up in the declaration that "a deal is a deal."

Japanese and certain other cultural groups consider that the goal of negotiation is not a signed contract but a relationship between the two sides. Although the written contract expresses the relationship, the essence of their deal is the relationship itself. For the American, signing a contract is closing a deal; for the Japanese, signing a contract might more appropriately be called opening a relationship. As will be seen, these differing goals can affect certain other aspects of the negotiating process.

If a "relationship" negotiator sits on the other side of the table, you need to be aware that merely convincing him of your ability to deliver on a low-cost contract will not get you the deal. You have to convince him instead, from the very first meeting, that your two organizations have the potential to build a rewarding relationship over the long term. On the other hand, if the other side is basically a "contract" deal maker, trying to build a relationship may be a waste of time and energy.

2. Negotiating Attitude: Win/Lose or Win/Win?

Because of culture or personality, or both, businesspersons appear to approach deal making with one of two basic attitudes: that a negotiation is either a process through which both can gain (win/win) or a process through which, of necessity, one side wins and the other loses (win/lose). As you enter negotiations, it is important to know which type of negotiator is sitting across the table from you. If one side has much greater bargaining power than the other, the weaker side has a tendency to see the negotiation as a win/lose situation: every gain for the powerful side is automatically a loss for the weaker party. As one Indian executive put it, "Negotiations between the weak and the strong are like negotiations between the lamb and the lion. Invariably, the lamb gets eaten." Win/win negotiators see deal making as a collaborative and problem-solving process; win/lose negotiators view it as confrontational.

Developing-country officials often view their negotiations with large multinational corporations as win/lose competitions. For example, in negotiating investment contracts, they sometimes take the view that any profits earned by the investor are automatically losses to the host country. As a result, they may focus rather fixedly in negotiations on limiting investor profit in contrast to discovering how to maximize the benefits from the project to both the investor and the host country.

The presence of a win/lose deal maker on the other side may block any deal. Searching constantly for the negative implications of every proposal while failing to evaluate the positive side, this type of negotiator may simply take a position and refuse to budge. How should you negotiate with a win/lose deal maker?

First, without appearing to condescend, explain fully the nature of the proposed transaction. Do not assume that the other side has the same degree of business sophistication as you. Part of their intransigence may stem from lack of understanding of the deal and an unwillingness to show ignorance.

Second, try to find out the other side's real interests — what do they really want out of the deal? Negotiators who encourage the other side to provide information about themselves, their interests, and their preferences generally achieve better results than those who do not. To do this you have to look behind the positions they take at the table. Here, the question is your most powerful tool. But questioning at the negotiating table requires a high degree of sophistication. On the one hand, you do not want to appear ignorant and therefore reduce your credibility with the other side. On the other, you do not want to seem indiscreet by appearing to ask for business secrets. Many foreign companies attach a much greater importance to secrecy than do American corporations, which have to contend daily with the disclosure requirements of U.S. law and business practice. For example, although the salary of the chairman of a U.S. publicly traded corporation is a matter of public record, the salary of the president of a French corporation is a tightly kept secret. The cultural differences on what is and what is not considered secret can complicate information exchange, which is so vital to determining interests. But one principle that all cultures seem to respect is reciprocity. If you are open and provide information easily, the other side will be led to provide you with information. Your own openness may be the best way to get persons across the table to open up.

Third, to understand the other side's interests, you need to know something about its history and culture. For instance, Mexico's history of domination by the United States invariably leads Mexican corporations to pursue both profits and prestige in their negotiations with American companies. A lucrative deal that places a Mexican corporation in a visible second-class position will probably fail.

And finally, once you have been able to identify the other side's interests, you have to develop proposals directed at satisfying those interests. Here, creativity and innovation are essential. In one negotiation between an American contractor and a foreign manufacturing corporation for the construction and sale of an electrical cogeneration plant, the foreign negotiators insisted that if the plant did not work up to a specified standard, the American corporation would have to dismantle the entire plant and take it all away. The American company was unwilling to make that kind of guarantee. As the negotiations appeared to disintegrate, the American negotiators realized that the real interest of the foreign corporation was not in having a cogeneration plant but in having a reliable supply of electricity. The Americans therefore proposed that, if the plant was defective and could not be fixed, they would take over and run it, provided the foreign corporation agreed to purchase all the electricity it produced. Ultimately, the two sides struck a deal on this basis. An understanding of interests led to the creation of innovative proposals, which in turn led to a deal.

3. Personal Style: Informal or Formal?

An executive's "style" at the negotiating table is usually characterized as formal or informal. References to style focus on the way a negotiator talks to others, uses titles, dresses, speaks, and interacts with other persons. A negotiator with a formal style insists on addressing the other team by their titles, avoids personal anecdotes, and refrains from questions touching on the private or family life of members of the other side. An informal style of negotiator tries to start the discussion on a first-name basis, quickly seeks to develop a personal, friendly relationship with the other team, and may take off his jacket and roll up his sleeves when deal making begins in earnest. Each culture has its own formalities, which have special meaning. They are another means of communication among the persons sharing that culture. For an American or an Australian, calling someone by his first name is an act of friendship and therefore a good thing. In other cultures, such as the French, Japanese, or Egyptian, the use of a first name at a first meeting is an act of disrespect and therefore a bad thing.

Negotiators in a foreign culture must take care to respect appropriate formalities. As a general rule, it is always safer to adopt a formal posture and gradually move to an informal stance, if the situation warrants it, than to assume an informal style too quickly. Degrees of appropriate formality vary from culture to culture. As an illustration, in the Sudan, an Arab country, informality is more readily and quickly tolerated than in Egypt, its Arab neighbor down the Nile.

4. Communication: Direct or Indirect?

Methods of communication vary among cultures. Some place emphasis on direct and simple methods of communication; others rely heavily on indirect and complex methods. The latter may use circumlocutions, figurative forms of speech, facial expressions, gestures, and other kinds of body language. In a culture that values directness, such as the German, you can expect to receive a clear and definite response to questions and proposals. In cultures that rely on indirect communication, reaction to your proposal may be gained only by interpreting a series of signs, gestures, and seemingly indefinite comments. What you will not receive at a first meeting is a definite commitment or rejection.

The presence of conflict in a negotiation may lead to the use of extreme forms of indirect communication. In one case, a small U.S. manufacturing concern located in New York was having difficulty paying its Japanese suppliers, who had been asking for their money without success for some time. The American company was allied with a Canadian partner for certain business in Canada. One day the Japanese called the Canadian and asked to meet with him at his office in Toronto, to which the Canadian agreed. When the Japanese arrived for the meeting, they asked where John, the owner of the American company, was. Surprised, the Canadian replied that he had had no idea that they wanted to see John. They said they did and asked the Canadian if he would mind calling John to invite him to Toronto for a meeting with them. After receiving the call, John flew to Toronto for discussions about his financial problems. The Japanese indirectly brought about the meeting that they were reluctant to arrange directly.

5. Sensitivity to Time: High or Low?

Discussions of national negotiating styles invariably treat a particular culture's attitudes toward time. So it is said that Germans are always punctual, Mexicans are habitually late, Japanese negotiate slowly, and Americans are quick to make a deal. Commentators claim that some cultures "value" time more than others, but this may not be an accurate characterization of the situation. Rather, they value differently the amount of time devoted to and measured against the goal pursued. For Americans, the deal is a "signed contract" and "time is money," so they want to make a deal quickly. Americans therefore try to reduce formalities to a minimum and get down to business. For members of other cultures, who view the purpose of the negotiation as creating a relationship rather than simply signing a contract, there is a need to invest time in the negotiating process so that the parties can get to know one another well and determine whether they wish to embark on a long-term relationship. Aggressive attempts to shorten the negotiating time may be viewed by the other side as efforts to hide something and therefore may be a cause of distrust. These elements should be taken into account in planning and scheduling negotiation sessions and in dealing with other factors affecting the pace of negotiations.

6. Emotionalism: High or Low?

Accounts of negotiating behavior of persons from other cultures almost always point to a particular group's tendency or lack thereof to act emotionally. According to the stereotype, Latin Americans show their emotions at the negotiating table, but Japanese hide their feelings. Obviously, individual personality plays a role here. There are passive Latins and hot-headed Japanese. But various cultures have different rules as to the appropriateness of displaying emotions, and these rules are usually brought to the negotiating table as well.

7. Form of Agreement: General or Specific?

Cultural factors also influence the form of agreement that parties try to make. Generally, Americans prefer very detailed contracts that attempt to anticipate all possible circumstances, no matter how unlikely. Why? Because the "deal" is the contract itself, and one must refer to the contract to determine how to handle a new situation that may arise. Other cultures, such as that of China, prefer a contract in the form of general principles rather than detailed rules. Why? Because, it is claimed, the essence of the deal is the relationship of trust that exists between the parties. If unexpected circumstances arise, the parties should look to their relationship, not the contract, to solve the problem. So in some cases, the American drive at the negotiating table to foresee all contingencies may be viewed by persons from another culture as evidence of lack of confidence in the stability of the underlying relationship.

Some persons argue that differences over the form of an agreement are caused more by unequal bargaining power between the parties than by culture. In a situation of unequal bargaining power, the stronger party always seeks a detailed agreement to "lock up the deal" in all its possible dimensions, while the weaker party prefers a general agreement to give it room to "wiggle out" of adverse circumstances that are almost bound to occur in the future. So a Chinese commune as the weaker party in negotiations with a multinational corporation will seek a general agreement as a way of protecting itself against the future. According to this view, it is not culture but context that determines this negotiating trait.

American companies usually prefer to arrive at a detailed, comprehensive contract. Companies in some other countries do, too. The Russians, it is said, invariably live up to the letter of an agreement, but have a tendency to ignore oral or tacit agreements they may have made. Consequently, most experienced deal makers stress the need to pay careful attention to the written word in negotiating in the countries of the former Soviet Union. One U.S. executive recalls an instructive experience from the days of détente in the early 1970s, when he negotiated a major deal with a Soviet foreign trade organization. The negotiations had taken place in both New York and Moscow and extended over two years. In what was to be the last day of the last session, at three o'clock in the morning, after the technical experts on both sides had gone to bed, the two team leaders, with their lawyers, were reviewing the final document. The Soviet team leader casually suggested adding a clause beginning with the word ''however'' to clarify a payment term. Rather than accept or reject the clause directly, the U.S. team leader woke up all the technical experts and had them review the entire four-hundred-page document to determine the impact of the proposed clause. After three hours of study, they concluded that the clause would cost the U.S. company $200 million in an adverse market. The American executive rejected the proposal. Ironically, he recalled an earlier conversation with the Soviet negotiator while they were watching a speech on television by President Richard Nixon. ''You know,'' said the Soviet, ''watching Nixon is a lot like reading *Pravda:* when you come to a 'however,' you'd better look out!''

8. Building an Agreement: Bottom Up or Top Down?

Related to the form of an agreement is the question of whether negotiating a business deal is an *inductive* or *deductive* process. Does it start from agreement on general principles and proceed to specific items, or does it begin with agreement on specifics, such as price, delivery date, and product quality, the sum total of which becomes the contract? Different cultures tend to emphasize one approach over the other.

Some observers believe that the French prefer to begin with agreement on general principles, while Americans tend to seek agreement first on specifics. For Americans, negotiating a deal is basically making a whole series of compromises and trade-offs on a long list of particulars. For the French, the essence is to agree on basic general principles that will guide and indeed determine the negotiation process afterward. The agreed-upon general principles become the framework, the skeleton, upon which the contract is built.

A further difference in negotiating style is seen in the dichotomy between the "building down" approach and the "building up" approach. In the building-down approach, the negotiator begins by presenting a maximum deal if the other side accepts all the stated conditions. In the building-up approach, one side starts by proposing a minimal deal that can be broadened and increased as the other party accepts additional conditions. According to many observers, Americans tend to favor the building-down approach, while the Japanese prefer the building-up style of negotiating a contract.

9. Team Organization: One Leader or Group Consensus?

In any international business negotiation, it is important to know how the other side is organized, who has the authority to make commitments, and how decisions are made. Culture is one important factor that affects the way executives organize themselves to negotiate a deal. One extreme is the negotiating team with a supreme leader who has complete authority to decide all matters. Americans tend to follow this approach, described as the "John Wayne style of negotiations":[2] one person has all the authority and plunges ahead to do a job, and to do it as quickly as possible. Other cultures, notably the Japanese and the former Soviets, stress team negotiation and consensus decision making. When you negotiate with such a team, it may not be apparent who is the leader and who has the authority to commit the side. In the first type, the negotiating team is usually small; in the second, it is often large. For example, in negotiations in China on a major deal, it would not be uncommon for the Americans to arrive at the table with three persons and for the Chinese to show up with ten. Similarly, the one-leader team is usually prepared to make commitments and decisions more quickly than a negotiating team organized on the basis of consensus. As a result, the consensus type of organization usually takes more time to negotiate a deal.

10. Risk Taking: High or Low?

Studies seem to support the idea that certain cultures try to avoid risk more than others.[3] In any given deal, the willingness of one side to take "risks" in the negotiation process — to divulge information, to be open to new approaches, to tolerate uncertainties in a proposed course of action — can be affected by the personality of the negotiator and the context of the negotiation. Nonetheless, there are certain cultural traits to this effect. The Japanese, with their emphasis on requiring enormous amounts of information and on their intricate group decision-making process, tend to be risk adverse. Americans, by comparison, are risk takers.

If you determine that the team on the other side of the table is risk adverse, focus your attention on proposing rules, mechanisms, and relationships that will reduce the apparent risks in the deal for them.

Type A and Type B Negotiators

Negotiating styles, like personalities, have a wide range of variation. The ten negotiator traits listed above and the range of variation within each trait easily show the complexity of the problem. For purposes of simplification one might divide negotiators into two types, A and B, just as a famous cardiology study grouped the human race into type A and type B personalities. The following table may be helpful in identifying the two types.

TRAIT	TYPE A NEGOTIATOR		TYPE B NEGOTIATOR
Goal	Contract	↔	Relationship
Attitudes	Win/Lose	↔	Win/Win
Personal Styles	Informal	↔	Formal
Communications	Direct	↔	Indirect
Time Sensitivity	High	↔	Low
Emotionalism	High	↔	Low
Agreement Form	Specific	↔	General
Agreement Building	Bottom-up	↔	Top-down
Team Organization	One leader	↔	Consensus
Risk-taking	High	↔	Low

Unlike the purpose of the cardiology study, the purpose of this categorization is not to argue that one type is better than another or to persuade a type A negotiator to become more like a type B negotiator. Individual negotiators may not fit neatly into either of these two categories. While Americans may tend to be type A and Japanese type B, Russians, Germans, and Poles may have negotiating traits that draw from both types. The purpose of the checklist is to identify the specific cultural and personality characteristics that affect deal making, and to show the possible variation that a particular trait may take. With this knowledge, a global deal maker is better prepared to cope with the complexities of culture in an international business negotiation.

4

Ducking Ideologies

DEAL MAKERS take not only their cultures to the table, but also their political beliefs. Probe deeply enough into the mind of even the most apolitical executive, and you will find an ideology, a more or less systematic body of beliefs that explains how society works and what program of political action it should follow. Far from being merely political baggage, ideologies define right and wrong, direct human conduct toward specific goals, and inspire social change. Communism, capitalism, socialism, nationalism, fascism, Peronism, Maoism, Nasserism, and Islamic fundamentalism are just a few of the many ideologies that the world has had to contend with over the last fifty years. Throughout that time numerous conflicting ideologies have also been a constant feature of the international business scene.

American managers, whether they are Republicans or Democrats, generally share a common ideology, so ideological differences rarely complicate domestic deal making. Once Americans enter the global arena, however, they encounter ideologies vastly different from their own. The presence of different ideologies at the negotiating table can be a real barrier to making a deal. This chapter examines the nature of that barrier, its impact on the negotiation process, and ways of overcoming it. As a general rule, global deal makers should try to avoid ideology at the negotiating table.

The Elements of Ideology

Ideology is deadly serious business. Whether it is socialism or capitalism, nationalism or Islamic fundamentalism, ideology gives authoritative answers to some basic questions. What should be the relationship between the individual and the community? How should that relationship be guaranteed and enforced? How should the means of producing goods and services be organized and governed? What should be the role of the state in the lives of its citizens? How should the state and its citizens treat the citizens of other states?

No two ideologies answer all these questions precisely alike. Each ideology has its own explanation of what is good and bad in society; each has its own approach to fixing things. The answers to these questions, of course, are essential background in putting together any business deal.

Some American managers tend to think of ideologies in sweeping, general categories: capitalism, socialism, nationalism. But these categories are much too broad to guide deal makers in foreign countries. Existing ideologies in a particular country have usually been adapted to suit that country's particular needs. The socialism of China is different from that of North Korea, and the capitalism of the United States is different from that of Canada.

Numerous factors shape and influence a particular ideology. Internal factors, such as a country's geography, demography, culture, and resources are powerful forces in shaping an ideology. Thus Japan's dense population, island structure, poor resource base, and homogeneous ethnic background have given it a communitarian ideology that emphasizes the importance of cooperating for the common good. Similarly, external forces such as colonialism and invasion also play a role. Latin America's history of outside domination has surely prompted the strong nationalist ideology that prevails throughout the continent.

Ideology may be identified with a particular culture or nationality, but it is distinct from both. Some countries with a more or less unified culture are nevertheless ideologically divided. France, for example, has two basic ideological tendencies—one left and one right—which date back to the French Revolution of 1789. As a result there is no single French ideology, although a single French culture and a single French nationality do exist. And in many Arab countries, like Egypt, one can find ideologies of Western capitalism, Arab socialism, and Islamic fundamentalism sitting side by side (however uneasily) in the same office.

Ideology and the Deal-making Process

Ideology has a dual impact on global deals: it affects the negotiation process and it influences the nature of the transaction ultimately agreed upon. Ideological differences between two sides can complicate the deal-making process in numerous ways.

First, ideologies have an adversarial quality. They have their good guys and bad guys, friends and foes, right and wrong ways. Thus ideological differences at the negotiating table can increase mistrust between the parties and raise suspicions about the other side's intentions, honesty, and reliability. As a result, the parties may come to see themselves not as jointly engaged in solving a business problem, but as ideological adversaries to be watched very carefully.

Second, ideological differences can complicate communication between deal makers. The use of ideological jargon may seem natural and value-free to a person holding that ideology, but it often appears provocative to the other side. An American executive may consider "free enterprise," "profit," and "private property" to be unquestionably good things; however, an Argentinean government official or Chinese manager may consider them more ambivalently.

Third, ideology may lead negotiators to take hard-and-fast positions. As a result, they may obstruct the process of shaping an agreement by exploring areas of mutual interests and developing creative options to advance them. In the negotiation of a joint venture in a developing country, the local government may insist on 51 percent ownership for reasons of nationalism requiring that enterprises be under local control. Although the purpose behind its position on ownership is to assure local control, ideology may prevent the government from exploring ways for controlling the enterprise without owning 51 percent of its shares. For instance, it might hold a class of shares with more voting power than that owned by its foreign partner.

Ideology and the Substance of the Deal

Ideology, of course, can also complicate the substance of a deal itself. Three areas of ideological difference often faced by U.S. negotiators are private investment, profit, and individual rights. Americans tend to view private investment as a positive good, a force to create wealth, jobs, useful products, and income; however, many foreign countries look at investment more circumspectly. For them, investment—particularly foreign investment—has its benefits and its costs, and host countries seek to maximize the benefits and minimize the costs through government regulation. Profit is also viewed differently. For Americans, profit results from growth and is good because it can be reinvested to yield further profits. In other countries, the profits one person gains are wealth taken from somebody else. Similarly, Americans stress the rights of the individual, but other nationalities, like the Chinese, emphasize the rights of the group.

Aside from these individual issues, the ideology of nationalism is a constant theme, sometimes muted, sometimes blatant in many if not most international business negotiations. Its presence at the table is basically defensive—to thwart a proposal that might harm national interests and sovereignty. It can take many forms. Sometimes, as in Japan, it is a general but unstated barrier to foreign penetration of the local market. In other places, like Latin America, it may be embodied in a specific law or doctrine, such as the Calvo doctrine, which prohibits local organizations from agreeing to submit business disputes to international arbitration, because this would give foreigners the privilege of avoiding national courts.

Dealing with Ideologies

How should you deal with the barrier of ideology at the negotiating table? The basic strategy to follow is avoidance. You will not change the other side's ideology, and they will certainly not change yours. Therefore, if you really want to make a global deal, you must duck ideology.

That piece of advice is not as easy to put into practice as it sounds. The following are eight simple rules you should observe for ducking ideology.

1. *Know your own ideology.* American executives tend to think of themselves as pragmatists. They have viewpoints, even philosophies. But few self-respecting corporate executives believe they have an ideology. The ideologies are on the other side of the table. They, not we, are the zealots and the fanatics.

That reaction is self-delusion. We all have ideologies. We all have answers to the basic questions raised earlier in this chapter, questions that every ideology tries to answer. And even if our political beliefs seem to us to be obvious and eternal truths, acknowledged by mankind as laws of nature, those beliefs will inevitably appear to be an ideology to somebody on the other side of the negotiation table. Thus you should also try to understand how the other side views the ideology that you hold.

2. *Once you have learned your own ideology, don't preach it.* You are at the table to make deals, not converts. Trumpeting your own ideology may antagonize the other side. At the very least, your gratuitous praise of "free enterprise" in a socialist country will be interpreted to be criticism of the country's prevailing ideology. Do not transform a business negotiation into an ideological struggle. Even in these days, when capitalism seems to have won over communism as an economic system, becoming a missionary for capitalism, rather than focusing on your job as a business negotiator, may lose you a deal in the end.

3. *Know the other side's ideology and take it seriously.* Ideology, like culture, gives you important insights into the other side. You should therefore seek to understand that ideology and how it came about.

One way you can begin to gain that knowledge is by reading a modern political history of the country in which you want to do business. Local newspapers and magazines and discussions with embassy officials and your consultants can also be extremely helpful in this respect. Of course, members of the other negotiating team, often in social conversation, can give important information on the prevailing ideology in the country, as well as on their own political beliefs.

Understanding the other side's ideology helps you to understand its interests. Once you understand interests, you can begin to shape an acceptable deal. In one socialist country a major U.S. soft-drink producer wanted to set up a bottling plant and distribution network. The prevailing ideology in the country stressed the importance of the group over the individual, and the need to develop industrial capacity at the expense of consumer goods. Soft drinks hardly seemed to fit the country's ideological priorities. Indeed, one government official dismissed the product as a "useless drink." Eventually a deal was struck, but not on the basis that the drink would satisfy the local population's thirst. Instead, the U.S. negotiators justified the project on the ground that it would contribute to the country's industrial development. The project was restructured to include a heavy training component for local workers and managers, as well as a farm where certain ingredients would be grown. In addition, the U.S. manufacturer promised to make efforts to persuade other American companies to consider investments in the country.

Americans not only feel that they themselves have no ideology, but they also tend to believe that the proclaimed ideologies of other persons are not genuine. For many U.S. executives, ideological statements merely justify interests. They assume that foreign business executives and officials just parrot the ideological line to get along with their governments: nobody really believes that stuff.

It is dangerous to arrive at the negotiating table with that attitude. It is far better to assume that negotiators on the other side believe the ideological line they are giving you — at least until you have direct evidence that they don't.

4. *Look for ideological divisions on the other side.* In negotiating any deal you have to be concerned about the other side's ideology at three different levels: personal, organizational, and national. Specifically, you need to determine: (1) the ideology of the persons you are negotiating with; (2) the ideology of the organization you hope to make a deal with; and (3) the ideology prevailing in the country where you want to do business.

In many but not all instances, the ideologies at the three levels are the same. It sometimes happens that the personal, organizational, and national ideologies of the other side are all different, even inconsistent. These differences in ideology may either facilitate or complicate deal making. For example, if a foreign executive with whom you are negotiating is clearly not sympathetic to his country's prevailing socialist ideology, the opportunity to make a deal may be greater than if he were a genuine socialist. However, if a country has a declared open-door policy toward foreign investment, but the official with whom you are negotiating holds strong nationalist and socialist views, making a deal on a foreign investment project may prove to be difficult.

U.S. companies discovered the problem created by ideological diversity in the 1970s, when Egypt, under President Anwar Sadat, actively tried to promote foreign investment. Despite favorable policies and laws, prospective investors in Egypt encountered significant barriers in the offices of government agencies and state corporations. Officials in those offices had formed a set of beliefs, known as Arab Socialism, during the previous twenty years under the rule of President

Gamal Nasser. As a result, they came to view foreign investors as a threat to Egypt's sovereignty and to existing public-sector companies. The arrival of a new president, with new laws and policies, did not cause them to put aside those beliefs suddenly. So regardless of Sadat's speeches inviting foreign capital to Egypt, many Egyptian officials continued to bring their old ideology to the table and therefore obstructed deal making. To counter this situation, American companies sought to shift negotiations to a higher level in the bureaucracy, where they felt they would find an ideology more in tune with what they were hearing from President Sadat.

5. *Avoid discussion of ideological positions and focus instead on interests.* If a country has taken a strong ideological position on an issue, say, the predominance of public-sector enterprise over that of the private sector, it does little good to try to persuade officials of that country that its position is wrong. Rather, try to determine the goals that the other side is pursuing through that ideological position, then seek to propose options that will enable that side to achieve those goals. In the case of the soft-drink plant in the socialist country, it would have been confrontational and counterproductive for the U.S. company to have tried to persuade the government to provide more goods for consumers. Instead, it identified the country's interests in developing its industrial capacity and convinced the government that the soft-drink plant, distribution system, and farm would help the country to advance its interests.

6. *Look for the gaps between ideology and reality.* As we have seen in Eastern Europe, reality changes faster than ideology. With that change, a gap develops between the two as ideology's explanation of society and its proposed solutions seem more and more inadequate. Eventually, when the gap

becomes too great, the prevailing ideology is abandoned or reformed. Thus, when communism became less and less relevant to the problems of East Germany, it was discarded as that country's prevailing ideology.

Similarly, as deal makers come to know a country, they should seek to identify gaps between ideology and the realities of the local business and economic environment. The existence of large gaps between ideology and reality may provide business opportunities and suggest areas in which official ideology is less of an obstacle to deal making. For example, if the ideology of a state stresses the importance of the group over the individual, but the role of the individual is increasing in the society, opportunities for business deals in consumer goods may arise. Then, too, the existence of big gaps between official ideology and the social realities may mean that major political changes will soon take place.

7. *Try to structure deals around ideological obstacles.* Often ideological principles crystalize into laws, rules, and institutions that threaten to block deals. Nationalism requires that all natural resources belong to the state, and that no one else can own them. Islamic fundamentalism prohibits interest payments on loans. Egyptian socialism demands that workers participate both in the management and in the profits of an enterprise. Each of these principles can be an obstacle to deal making in particular cases. Yet, with some creativity, it is possible to structure a deal in such a way that the ideological principle is respected, but business goes forward. A loan to a project might be secured by its assets and paid for by an annual administrative fee and a percentage of the profits in lieu of interest. A petroleum development contract could be written in such a way that ownership of the oil is transferred not when the oil is in the ground, but at the point where it leaves the flange of the well.

And worker participation in management need not mean a seat on the board of directors but merely an advisory committee that meets regularly with an officer of the company.

Some countries, such as the former Soviet Union, appear to have an ideological aversion to paying for services, especially at the going international rates. Influenced by their own egalitarian wage structure, they often resisted paying high fees for engineering, technical, and managerial services. One way of dealing with this kind of ideological barrier is to repackage a deal as a sale of a product rather than of services alone: the provision of management services to a new factory could be included as part of the contract of sale for the factory instead of being spelled out in a separate contract.

8. *Maintain confidentiality.* The more public the negotiations, the more likely that ideological differences will surface. In the glare of publicity, local executives and officials feel a strong need to show to the government, the public, and their colleagues that they are adhering to appropriate ideological positions. For example, in a mineral negotiation that receives a great deal of publicity, the officials representing the host country may feel obliged to show that they are not selling out to foreigners. As a result, their positions may harden, and they may prove to be inflexible at the table.

Executives should therefore seek to establish and maintain confidentiality in negotiations as one way of softening the influence of ideology. To create a confidential atmosphere, the U.S. team should be careful in what they say to others outside the negotiating room. They should naturally avoid comments to the press and indeed should specifically agree that the host country side will be the principal source of public commentary on the negotiations. Another way to foster confidentiality, as chapter 2 pointed out, is to hold discussions in another country or some out-of-the-way site.

Sometimes You Don't Need to Duck

Ideology is not always a barrier. Sometimes it may be a positive force in negotiating and carrying out a deal. The legendary commitment of Japanese employees to their firm may be just as useful to a foreign company operating in Japan as to a native Japanese corporation.

In negotiating a settlement following the nationalization of its interests in Zaire, a U.S. oil company saw the positive side of ideology. It was concerned that the Zaire government would claim ownership of the company's international trademarks, which were registered locally in the name of the company's nationalized subsidiary. Early in the discussions, the company realized that the government, for nationalist ideological reasons, wanted to reduce the visibility of foreign multinational corporations in the country and to develop the image of its state-owned corporation. For that reason, it really did not want to use the U.S. oil company's trademarks. At the same time, the government did not have the resources to create its own trademarks, so chances were high that it would continue to use those of the oil company. Recognizing the government's ideological interests, the company commissioned a graphic artist to design and produce signs for the new Zaire state oil company and presented them to the government. The government was delighted to use them, and the company's international trademarks were protected. As this case demonstrates, wise negotiators constantly try to understand how to use the prevailing local ideology to their own advantage.

5

Bucking Foreign Bureaucracies

GLOBAL DEALS link organizations. Behind any international business negotiation are the companies, partnerships, government agencies, and state corporations whose interests are being discussed at the table. Deal makers are supposed to represent organizations, not act for themselves. Their job is to find a way to get their organizations to agree on a business relationship. Although deal making is an intensely personal activity driven by the personality, skill, and experience of individual negotiators, it is also a bureaucratic activity strongly influenced by the nature of the organizations involved.

As a business negotiator, you therefore not only have to be concerned about the persons sitting across the table from you, but you must also think constantly about the organizations and bureaucracies behind *them*. Those organizations can become barriers to deal making. Whether you are negotiating with a Chinese trading company, a Dutch multinational corporation, or an international consortium of Arab banks, making global deals is very much a process of engaging and dealing with foreign organizations—of bucking foreign bureaucracies.

The Importance of the Right Approach

For a tennis player, the right approach to the ball is essential to making a shot. For a diver, the right approach on the board can mean a graceful entry into the water as opposed to an embarrassing splash. So, too, the right approach to a foreign organization can be the difference between making a deal or walking away with empty hands. Instead of merely plunging ahead like an enthusiastic but uncoordinated ten-year-old leaping into a swimming pool, the wise deal maker seeks to answer a variety of questions and to consider numerous options *before* actually moving to engage a foreign organization in negotiations.

DO YOU HAVE THE RIGHT ONE?

In even the smallest country, a deal maker confronts many organizations. In most industries, a manager finds several companies. A fundamental question that must be answered before negotiations begin is: Have you identified the right one to make a deal with? Is this the company that can deliver what you want?

The question may appear elementary, even simplistic. But more than one U.S. executive has entered negotiations with a foreign company on the untested *assumption* that it could deliver the goods when in fact it could not. For example, representatives of a U.S. corporation spent several weeks discussing an agreement with a Korean firm to obtain the rights to manufacture an electronic device made by that firm, only to discover that the firm had no authority to license that technology outside Asia. Another Korean company held those rights.

IS ONE ENOUGH?

Even if the company you choose to deal with can deliver the goods, you may have to negotiate with other organizations to make the deal effective. Sometimes you have to bring them to the table and make them part of the agreement. At other times, you are better off dealing with them separately, as American executives did when negotiating a long-term purchase of natural gas from Algeria. They had to be careful in choosing which Algerian ministries to talk with and to avoid being caught in fights between the Ministry of Energy and the Ministry of Foreign Affairs. In the same vein, investors in the Sudan seeking to develop an agroindustrial project, like a sugar plantation and refinery, sometimes found themselves in the middle of conflicts between the Ministry of Agriculture and the Ministry of Industry as to which had control over the undertaking. Because of the intense jealousy between the two ministries, investors preferred to deal with each one separately, since that approach made each ministry feel it had primary authority over agroindustrial projects.

The potential for bureaucratic conflict is almost always present, and the global deal maker should be on the watch for it constantly. The risk is particularly high when one of the parties on the other side is a government agency or department. If you leave an important party out of negotiations, the omission may kill or at least delay a deal. Much time has to be spent in soothing hurt feelings, and the neglected organization invariably feels the need to be difficult to show its importance. It is not likely to come running to the negotiation table just because you belatedly extend an invitation.

HAVE YOU FOUND THE RIGHT BRANCH?

Often it is not enough just to negotiate with the right organization; you must be sure that you are dealing with the right branch of that organization. For example, if you are seeking an alliance with a subsidiary of a decentralized conglomerate, it may be pointless to try negotiations with group headquarters rather than the subsidiary itself. On the other hand, in a highly centralized corporate structure, it may be essential to negotiate certain deals with the parent company.

In one case, high-level officials from a ministry in the Soviet Union on a visit to the United States met with executives of an American organization and strongly urged them to begin negotiating a deal with two institutions under the ministry's control. Shortly after, the ministry sent a formal invitation to the Americans to visit Moscow, and the Soviet embassy in Washington also made encouraging noises. Convinced of the Soviets' readiness to deal, the Americans sent a team of executives to Moscow.

Ministry officials hosted a first meeting between the Americans and the heads of the two organizations under the ministry's control. The two organization heads were polite but cool. They found a "problem" or a "difficulty" for each proposal put forward by the Americans. At the end of the day, nothing had been accomplished. That evening, at a reception, one of the American executives and a Soviet organization head, discovering that they had both spent considerable time in France, dismissed their translator and spoke directly to each other in French. As the two warmed up to each other, the American asked why the negotiations were going nowhere. The Soviet negotiator responded that the proposed deal had been dreamed up in the ministry, that he had not been consulted until two days earlier, and that the ministry expected his already constrained budget to finance the deal — something he refused to do. When the American asked about the high-level ministry officials who had been so encouraging, the organization head dismissed them with a wave of his hand. "Them? They're generals without armies. We've got the machinery and the people. It's our budget, not theirs. If you want to do business, you've got to deal directly with us."

LEARNING BUREAUCRACY

Only with careful study can you tell whether you have (1) the right organization, (2) the right branch of the organization, and (3) all the organizations necessary to make a deal. Rather than plunge into negotiations with the hope of "learning as you go," invest time and resources, *before you go to the negotiating table*, on getting to know the organization with which you hope to make a deal.

In addition to understanding its finances and technology, you should also seek to learn its organizational and bureaucratic nature. That investigation should analyze its structure to discover where various functions and tasks are performed in the hierarchy. It should also examine the nature of the organization's leadership, the way decisions are implemented internally, the background of its senior management, and its relationships with its client and supporting organizations.

Where will you find this information? Much of what you need is not to be found in published documents. Few countries publish as much about their companies as the United States does. To a large extent, you will find your most valuable source of information in persons who have dealt with the organization. Companies that have already negotiated deals with the organization can be extremely helpful. Multinational banks, the

U.S. embassy, resident representatives of international agencies, lawyers, business consultants, and local companies can give you varying but important perspectives on the bureaucratic culture of the organization you are planning to approach. Once you gather this information, try to answer some basic questions that will help you decide on making your approach.

Will you be talking to the organization that will actually produce or deliver what you want?

If not, what assurances do you have that this organization can get it for you?

Within the country, what organizations and agencies will need to cooperate with the target organization to make the deal a success?

What is the nature of current relationships between the target organization and those other organizations and agencies?

If those relationships appear strong, what external factors might weaken those relationships during the course of the deal you hope to negotiate?

How does the target organization make decisions?

The answers to these questions are not only necessary to determine your approach to the target company, but they will also help you in actually conducting negotiations. Few organizations, outside the military, are monolithic structures in which orders are given at the top and all units obey instantly. Within an organization, whether public or private, some branches have more independence than others. As the Soviet case shows, some have a great deal of independence to make their own decisions. What this means, of course, is that within virtually all organizations, decision making by bureaucracies, public or private, requires a process of negotiation.

No company or agency is as monolithic as it may appear to

outsiders. As a result, making a global deal involves at least three separate, but linked, negotiations: those between you and the other side; those within the other organization; and those within your own organization.

One tactic used by experienced deal makers is to attempt to influence the other side's internal negotiations as a way to affect its behavior in its external negotiations. In order to pursue this tactic, you must not only understand the team across the table, but you must also know something about the other side's organization and how its bureaucracy operates. Should you learn that the other side's organization is badly divided over what it wants out of the deal under consideration, that information may lead you to restructure your proposal or drop out of negotiations entirely in preference to wasting time and money in a fruitless attempt to persuade what you assumed was a united organization.

Once you enter the international arena, you will find a wide variety of organizations and bureaucratic cultures. Each one presents particular challenges to deal making. Some organizations, like many Japanese corporations, arrive at a decision through a slow and painstaking process of internal building of consensus. They have large staffs that demand massive amounts of information, and they take what appears to be an inordinate amount of time to react to your proposals. Other companies, such as those headed by a Saudi entrepreneur, may present quite different bureaucratic problems. Building consensus within the organization is not necessary because the Saudi head makes all the decisions. He is the person who has to be convinced. His assistants and advisers may have little real influence on his thinking. But he may travel a great deal, be reluctant to delegate authority, and see little point in maintaining what an American would consider to be a well-staffed office. As a result, negotiations may be complicated by difficulties in arranging meetings and in conducting regular communication between your company and his.

The Other Team

In negotiating a deal, you do not engage the other side's entire organization but only its negotiating team. The members of that team are usually your primary link to the other organization until the deal is made. Conversely, the other organization's primary link to you is its negotiating team. It is through its team that the other organization will gain information and form its judgments about you. Consequently, the negotiators on the other team control the information about the deal that flows to their bureaucracy. This position of control over information can give the negotiators power to influence their bureaucracy's decisions.

Members of the other side's bureaucracy may have different views about you and the deal you are trying to put together. Some may favor it; others may be opposed. Without adequate information, neither potential supporters nor potential opponents can act effectively to influence the bureaucracy's decision-making process. A negotiator who wants to make a deal often tries to deny information about the negotiations to potential opponents in his own company. If you feel that negotiations are going well, it may therefore be a good idea to allow the other team to be the only conduit of information to its bureaucracy. Providing additional information to the wrong quarters may cause problems for both you and the other negotiating team. In social or other events that bring you into contact with members of the other side's bureaucracy, you should therefore keep your comments to small talk and not inadvertently become another conduit for information—a conduit that undermines the position of the negotiators on the other side of the table. Even something like your telling an employee of the company that its negotiating team was being "extremely cooperative" might cause opponents of the deal to criticize its representatives for not being tough enough and for caving in to foreigners.

On the other hand, if negotiations are not going well because of the other team's intransigence or pursuit of its own interests, it may be useful to find a way to open another channel of communication to its bureaucracy. How and where you open that conduit will depend on the nature of the deal, the two organizations involved, and the existing relationships between executives on both sides.

Sometimes negotiators try to build a second channel at the top; sometimes they do it at the bottom. In one joint-venture negotiation between a French and an American company, the Americans believed that the French team was not accurately conveying American proposals to its headquarters. While negotiations ground on unproductively, the chairman of the American company scheduled a vacation in Cannes, where the French company president had a summer home, and he asked a mutual friend to invite them to the same reception. The two men met and had a quiet chat about their business plans. Soon both companies changed the heads of their negotiating teams, and the two companies eventually struck a deal.

In another negotiation between an American company and a Japanese corporation, the American bureaucracy was of two minds about the deal: the engineering people wanted the deal because it would give them excellent access to new technology, but the financial people were concerned about the deal's cost. Financial managers controlled the American negotiating team. Sensing that the financial managers were not giving the U.S.

company a complete picture of the technological potential of the deal, the Japanese company, through one of its engineers who had worked for several years in the United States, began to provide that information to a former colleague, who had been hired as an engineer in the American company. The American engineer, in turn, passed this information along to his engineering colleagues. The American company president, who was himself an engineer, then took over the negotiations and signed a contract with the Japanese firm.

The nature and size of a negotiating team may reflect something about the bureaucracy it represents. A large team across the table from you may indicate that the other side has a large number of bureaucratic units that feel they need to be represented so as to have their own direct channel of communication to the deal-making process. A small team, on the other hand, may indicate a centralized bureaucratic structure in which individual units have relatively little independence and autonomy.

WHAT IS THE COMPOSITION OF THE OTHER TEAM?

The kind of team you face will vary from country to country, from company to company, and from deal to deal. Negotiating a joint venture in China will bring you into contact with a team of ten or more officials whose specific responsibilities are vague and whose leader is difficult to identify. In a poor African developing country, the opposing team for the same type of transaction may consist of one or two bureaucrats who have had no experience in global dealing, but whose leader is a deputy minister with considerable power within the bureaucracy.

The precise team that you meet deserves considerable study.

In the very early stages of negotiation, you have to obtain answers to some important questions about the other team. The following is one of the most basic.

How Much Clout Does the Team Have?

International business negotiators do not act for themselves; they act for their companies and organizations. They are agents. You therefore need to know how much clout they have within their own organizations. Clout means not only authority in the legal sense to make commitments for their principals, but it also refers to their influence to persuade their own bureaucracies to accept a deal they have negotiated. Are the persons on the other side of the table decision makers or merely mouthpieces for faceless managers somewhere in the company's bureaucracy? The difference between a decision maker and a mouthpiece is clout.

Determining whether the other side has clout is not always easy. One must look to a variety of sources. First, try to gather information about the experience of other companies in negotiating with the organization that you are dealing with. Seniority of the negotiators may also reveal their influence within their own bureaucracies, as does the degree of respect that their colleagues show to them. Title and position in the organization may also give a clue to the clout they wield. You can begin learning these facts by asking who will be part of the negotiating team, what their titles are, and whom they represent. At the beginning of the first negotiating session, when introductions are made, give each member of the other side your business card and indicate that you would like to have each of theirs in return. While this formality may seem elemental, negotiators sometimes fail to do it and lose an excellent opportunity to identify all the members of the other team. As a way of securing additional information about the other team's members, you might begin the first negotiating session by briefly describing the background of each of your team's members. When you have finished, turn to the leader or spokesperson of the other team with an indication, subtle or otherwise, that you expect the same from them.

If the other team has clout, negotiations are likely to go more quickly than if it does not. A team with little clout has to check back with headquarters constantly, which can significantly slow the deal-making process. Then, too, you need to be very careful about making concessions to a mere mouthpiece because of the risk that the mouthpiece, having given you bland assurances about his own concessions, may later say, after checking with the home office, that your concessions are not sufficient. Your concessions have gained you nothing. Having showed your cards, you will be led to make more concessions. On the other hand, when you make reciprocal concessions to a person with clout, you have some confidence that if he feels the deal is good, headquarters will go along.

Who's in Charge?

A second important matter is to determine who is in charge of the negotiating team. Knowing the leader in many countries is to know the person you have to persuade to make the deal. Knowing the leader also lets you know whom to watch particularly to determine reactions to your proposals.

In some bureaucratic cultures, like the American, team leadership is evident from the title and behavior of the negotiators. In others, it is not. While the spokesperson for an American team is invariably its leader, the spokesperson for a Chinese team may have relatively little authority. The real leader of the team may merely sit quietly in the negotiating session and let others do the talking. In this type of situation, you need to look for clues. As an example, one experienced negotiator in

China has his own rule of thumb that the person who pours the tea for the others is the leader of the Chinese team. Often, if you get to know a junior member of the team, he can give you an idea of who the leader is and the relative importance of the other members. In other countries, perquisites such as a car and driver, office furnishings, or a personal assistant to carry papers and run errands may signal leadership status.

Just as it is important to know which person is the leader, it is also useful to understand what enabled that person to become the head of the negotiating team. Leadership qualities vary from country to country. The appointment as leader of a negotiating team may have been influenced by numerous factors, some of which have nothing to do with a person's technical competence in the matter under discussion. State enterprises in countries with an autocratic political system sometimes choose team leaders because of their political ties and loyalty to the regime in power. In certain parts of Latin America, social connections count a great deal in achieving business leadership positions. Coming from a ''good family'' may be more important than having an M.B.A.

Other countries, like Japan, may place greater emphasis on broad administrative experience in many departments of a company than on in-depth background in a single area such as finance or sales. Moreover, unlike most American business negotiators, the other team's leader, despite the appearance of age, may have had relatively few years' experience in business. In Japan and France, for example, one sometimes finds high corporate executives who have joined a company after a distinguished career in government. As a result, they bring with them to business negotiations the attitudes, habits, and practices common to civil servants, in contrast to those of managers who have had a lifelong career in business.

These differing bureaucratic backgrounds between American and foreign negotiators can create obstacles in making deals. In one negotiation the U.S. team was headed by an executive vice president for manufacturing who had begun his career many years earlier as an engineer with the company. The Japanese team was led by an experienced manager, a graduate in law of the University of Tokyo, who had held a wide variety of positions in his firm. The American, who insisted on directing all technical questions to the leader of the Japanese team, was dismayed when he did not receive detailed responses. He might more appropriately have addressed his comments to the Japanese team as a whole, which included two highly competent engineers. In another case, a U.S. team became frustrated with the leader of a French team, a graduate of the prestigious National School of Administration and a former inspector in the Ministry of Finance, who conducted business dealings as though they were diplomatic negotiations. The Americans might have been more tolerant of the approach had they been aware of the French manager's background.

Will the Team Remain Stable?

Making a deal may stretch over months or even years and require many meetings between the two teams. During that time the deal makers become educated about their transaction, about their companies, and about one another. Their shared knowledge and personal ties can help the two sides reach an agreement. Continuity of negotiating team members is therefore important and desirable.

Too often, however, negotiators are faced with a problem when the members of the other team keep changing. They start discussions on a deal with one manager, set a date for a subsequent session, and return only to find that the manager with whom they had made a promising start was replaced by another who knows virtually nothing about the proposed deal. This happened to a British multinational corporation that wanted to build a sugar refinery in the Sudan; it had to go through negotiations with five different Sudanese team leaders before it was able to sign a contract.

In most cases, the reason for the other team's instability is not a tactic to disconcert you, but a response to the demands of its own bureaucracy. Many small countries have extremely limited numbers of trained managers and officials. Those who gain some experience or prove their ability may be promoted rapidly or transferred to more pressing duties. Also, political shifts can have significant impact on both state corporations and private companies in many countries, with the result that experienced managers are fired, transferred, or led to seek better jobs elsewhere. For example, the lure of high-paying jobs in Saudi Arabia and the Persian Gulf during the oil boom of the 1970s meant that hundreds, perhaps thousands, of skilled negotiators left influential positions throughout the Middle East to work in the Arabian Peninsula. Government policies to privatize state enterprises and encourage the private sector have also produced bureaucratic instability in many countries as talented, experienced officials in government and state organizations left their jobs, often in the middle of negotiating a deal, to earn a larger salary someplace else.

The result of these trends is that in the process of negotiating a major deal over any significant period of time, you are liable to face a different set of representatives on the other side of the table each time you return for a session. This instability has various effects on deal making. On the one hand, it may give you an advantage because you have superior knowledge about the emerging transaction. That knowledge may allow you to dominate discussions when you are faced with a new team that understands little about a deal except what it has gleaned from a file. It may also allow you to reintroduce issues that you lost in earlier meetings.

On the other hand, a change in members of the other team can slow the process as they spend time learning from you about the deal and your company, an exercise that you have already gone through at length with their predecessors. And a new team may reopen issues that had been settled in your favor at earlier negotiating sessions.

Handling Instability

How do you handle the problem of instability of the other negotiating team? Here are a few simple suggestions.

1. You need to recognize the problem and try to estimate the likelihood of changes occurring and their possible impact on the progress of your deal. A change of a junior official in a ten-person Chinese team is not too significant. A change in a deputy minister leading a two-person team in Kenya may mean that negotiations have to start again from scratch.

2. Make a paper trail. Thoroughly document what happens at each negotiating session and send copies to every member of the other side's team.

3. Make it a point to get to know every member, no matter how junior, of the other side's team. A junior member may later become a senior member. A junior member who continues on an otherwise unstable team may eventually become its official memory. If he has confidence in you and your company, he will communicate that fact to his colleagues as they join the team.

4. Always bring extra copies of all previous letters, memorandums, and drafts to every meeting. The former mem-

bers of the other team may have taken their copies with them, and the new members may be unfamiliar with or unable to find the file.

5. Have patience. Showing annoyance at the other team's instability yields nothing productive. It is not the fault of the new members, who are doing their best to cope. Your expression of irritation only makes you appear unreasonable and undermines your credibility.

What's Their Agenda?

Negotiators are supposed to act only in the best interests of their company, their sole agenda being their company's agenda. Of course, executives at the table are also influenced by their personal goals and needs. As a result, they usually have two agendas, one organizational, the other personal. Unyielding rejection of your proposals may be the result of an objective judgment by a negotiator across the table that they are not in the best interests of his company. Or it may be prompted by a fear that his colleagues will accuse him of caving in to foreigners. Or he may be afraid that the deal, while good for the company as a whole, will be bad for his department or for him personally. As a result, as you evaluate the other side's team, try to determine the personal agendas of each member, and particularly of its leader.

That knowledge may help you make the deal, or it may tell you that further discussions are pointless. For instance, if you realize that a member of the other team is concerned that the proposed deal with your company may harm his department or lower his status in his company, this knowledge may prompt you to restructure the deal to reassure him. And should you learn, as one U.S. company did, that the negotiator on the other side had been through a series of failed negotiations and that another failure would cause him to lose face at home, this information may give you the confidence to stand firm behind your proposal and not offer concessions.

Who Wants a Payoff?

The extreme pursuit of a private agenda at a negotiating table can lead to bribery and corruption. The foreign official or executive who wants a personal payment to make a deal with you is, unfortunately, often to be found in many parts of the world. If you are confronted with such a situation, you must refuse. The Foreign Corrupt Practices Act imposes severe penalties on U.S. companies and persons who pay bribes to foreign officials. Moreover, indulging in bribery has a corrosive effect on your own company and employees.

Precisely *how* you handle a demand for a bribe can be the difference between making a deal and watching negotiations collapse. The following suggestions may be helpful.

1. Recognize that in many cultures gifts and payments are an essential part of building relationships between persons and groups. To reject abruptly and moralistically any suggested request for a gift may be interpreted as a rejection of the relationship that the other side considers necessary to doing business with you.

2. Explain that while you have great respect for your counterpart, you risk prosecution under the Foreign Corrupt Practices Act if you pay him. When a West African minister, during a break in a negotiating session, poetically told a U.S. executive that the minister was "the first tree in the forest and needed water," the American replied in friendly but blunt terms, "If I pay you, I'll go to jail." And certainly, considering the personal relationship they had developed during the negotiations, the official would not want to see that happen.

3. You might deflect a demand for a bribe by making a donation or providing a service that benefits the country or the

local community. Your company might build a playground for a school or a dispensary for a village, allowing the officials with whom you have been negotiating to take full credit for persuading you to make this gift. You might also sponsor free cultural events such as an art exhibition, a play, or a rock concert. If you choose to go this route, you must be absolutely sure that the payments you make do indeed go to finance these charitable and social activities, not into the pockets of local officials.

4. If corruption is pervasive within an organization with which you are dealing, you may have no other options than to walk away from the deal. If corruption is not pervasive, you might attempt to involve in the negotiation process persons or departments that are not corrupt with the hope that their presence will serve to control the behavior of the negotiator seeking a bribe. In negotiating a long-term sales contract with a manufacturer's representative who is signaling the need for a payoff, you might stress your concerns over technology or product quality and ask that appropriate members of the engineering division participate in the discussions. Another approach is to seek to build a channel of communication at another, you would hope, higher level in the other side's bureaucracy, then use that channel to persuade the company of the benefits of dealing with you.

6

Dealing with Foreign Governments and Laws

IN THIS AGE of globalization, borders still count. Despite the growth of global markets and international communications, the world is still made up of sovereign, independent countries, each with its own legal and political system. At last count, there were nearly 190 of those systems, not to mention many national subdivisions, like Quebec and Northern Ireland, with their own sets of laws and government agencies. What this means, of course, is that executives negotiating international business transactions must be prepared to confront and deal with a bewildering array of foreign governments and laws.

The Challenges of Foreign Governments and Laws

American companies have to cope with law and government all the time in the United States. They structure mergers in intricate ways to take advantage of the Internal Revenue Code. They hire lobbyists in Washington to convince senators to vote for laws favoring their industries. They entertain mayors to get city contracts. So what is really different about international business?

The difference is that making global deals forces American

executives and companies to cope with *foreign* governments and *foreign* laws. The fact that these systems are foreign creates three major challenges that the global deal maker does not face at home. First, foreign political and legal systems are not only different, they are largely unknown to a U.S. company seeking to do business abroad. For an inexperienced business executive, foreign law and politics are a mysterious "black box" whose inner workings are incomprehensible and often produce unpredictable results. Second, because the laws and government decisions of that country are equal to those of other countries, an American company in the international arena must deal with many different such systems, each equally authoritative. As a result, there is always the danger that the U.S. company may be "squeezed" between the law of the country in which it is trying to make a deal and that of the United States or any other country in which it has interests. Finally, foreigners in any legal and political system must always be concerned about unfair discrimination. Will they be subject to unfavorable decisions merely because they are foreigners? Will the courts treat them impartially in cases involving nationals of that country? Will they be able to compete on an equal footing with local businesses? Or will they be subject to the vagaries of "hometown justice"?

Foreign governments and laws are therefore another major barrier to the global deal, a barrier that takes many forms and shapes. To cope with foreign governments and laws effectively, negotiators must learn to deal with the problems of (1) the "black box," (2) the "squeeze," and (3) "hometown justice." This chapter treats each of these in turn.

The Black Box

Like cultures, each of the world's legal and political systems is distinct and different. The French government does not make policy the way the German government does. The laws and court procedures of India are distinct from those of England, even though India was part of the British empire for many years. And an American executive cannot assume that governments abroad work the way the U.S. government does at home.

A major U.S. manufacturer learned this lesson several years ago when it tried to put together a consortium of companies to produce for NATO a weapons system that it had already built successfully for the American military. Knowing the capabilities of various European companies, it selected those it thought could best do the job and began negotiating with them. These conversations were abruptly cut short when individual NATO governments told the U.S. manufacturer that they, not the American weapons company, would choose the European participants in the consortium. Recognizing political realities, the American company ended discussions with the companies it had selected, began negotiations with those chosen by the individual governments, and ultimately put together a consortium that successfully produced the weapons system for NATO.

A few years later, the same U.S. company, at the urging of the American government, sought to produce a version of the same weapons system for Japan. Having learned what it thought was a useful lesson from its earlier experience in Europe, it opened talks directly with the Japanese government, expecting it to indicate which Japanese companies the U.S. manufacturer was to work with, but no such indication was forthcoming. Japanese officials studiously avoided suggesting an appropriate Japanese partner. Finally, in a private conversation with the U.S. company's president, the Japanese deputy minister made it clear that the U.S. manufacturer, not the Japanese government, would decide on the Japanese company to participate in producing the weapons system. The reason was that two very powerful Japanese electronics firms were the primary contenders for participation, and the Japanese government did not want to incur the wrath and political antagonism of either one by choosing the other.

In both the European and Japanese cases, the "black box" of government processed a political decision, but each came out with a different result. In Europe, in matters of national defense, governments were dominant over industry. In Japan, the government, when faced with two competing electronics giants, clearly was not. With their knowledge of the workings of their governments, local business experts in both Europe and Japan probably could have predicted these results. Without that knowledge of the "black box" of government, an outsider, like the U.S. weapons manufacturer, could not.

GOVERNMENT INTEREST IN A DEAL?

It is important, in negotiating any international deal, to understand the position of the government of the country concerned toward that deal. Few countries, even the most stoutly capitalistic, are as open to business transactions by foreigners as is the United States. If a government senses that a proposed deal is not in its interest, it intervenes in the negotiation process or, if a contract has already been signed, takes actions to make its execution difficult, if not impossible. Thus, the first and most basic question for a global deal maker is whether the government of the country concerned has an interest in the transaction and will permit it to happen.

If the deal is permissible, you then need to find out exactly how it fits into the country's priorities. If a U.S. company is thinking about a joint venture in Romania to produce refrigerators for the local market, it must first discover, before starting serious negotiations with its local joint-venture partner, whether the Romanian government has targeted refrigerators as an area for foreign investment and what priority refrigerator manufacturing has among other economic activities in the country. If Romania's policies stress industrial equipment rather than consumer goods like refrigerators, the proposed joint venture may have a hard time securing the foreign exchange, tax benefits, and government permits it needs to go into production.

A careful reading of national development plans, economic policy statements, and related legislation can give an indication of national priorities. Conversations with government officials shed even greater light on the subject. But sometimes a country does not seem to have well-defined priorities. At first glance a U.S. executive may interpret the lack of stated priorities as a favorable openness to all sorts of business deals and investments, a reading that often proves wrong. In the economies of scarcity that exist in many countries, unstated priorities in relatively good times inevitably emerge in tough times when governments have to make hard decisions about allocating foreign exchange, energy, raw materials, and even space for freight in an antiquated railroad or port. The discovery of these priorities *after* a U.S. company has invested time and money in a deal can prove costly to the company if a government eventually decides that the proposed deal is not important. In planning any international deal, do not take the government's general statements of economic openness at face value. You need to make your own hardheaded analysis of how the government will react toward your deal in both good times and bad. One important way of getting this information is by talking to local businesspersons who have firsthand knowledge of how the government has reacted to economic hard times in the past.

SHOULD THE GOVERNMENT BE AT THE TABLE?

Once you have determined the nature of government interest in a transaction, you have to consider whether the government should be part of the deal. Should the government be at the negotiating table? The answer to this question depends on the kind of deal you are trying to make, the kind of economy you will have to operate in, and the kind of political system you will have to cope with.

An American company faced this problem in China when it negotiated a joint-venture agreement with a state-owned Chinese corporation to produce motor vehicles. To operate effectively, the new factory would need a supply of parts, but China had no plants to manufacture them. After the deal was signed and the factory constructed, the U.S. company applied to the Chinese government for foreign exchange to import the parts. The government, which had not signed the joint-venture agreement, felt under no obligation to provide foreign exchange for this purpose. As a result, a period of intense conflict between the government and the U.S. investor followed. Clearly, this was a case in which the government should have been brought to the negotiating table at the time the joint venture was being arranged so the partners could obtain a commitment to provide the needed foreign exchange for parts.

GOVERNMENTS FEEL DIFFERENT

Americans are often unprepared for the extensive—indeed, pervasive—role played by foreign governments in international business. Governments in many countries not only regulate economic activities and run public utilities as is fairly common in the United States, but they also participate actively, through ministries, state corporations, and government agencies, in all sorts of business activities from trading and insurance to manufacturing and agriculture.

In many nations government corporations have an exclusive monopoly over all imports entering the country and all exports leaving it. In fact, for American companies seeking major customers, agents, or joint-venture partners in many parts of the world, state corporations or government agencies are the only realistic possibility. As a result, deals that in the United States are made between private parties can be made abroad only with governments. Although the shift from planned to capitalist economies that has taken place in Eastern Europe and other parts of the world will reduce the role of government in business, state-owned corporations are destined to remain active players in global deal making.

Does the presence of a government at the table make a difference in negotiating a deal? Absolutely. According to one experienced international executive, "Negotiating with governments feels different." For one thing, deal making with state corporations and agencies involves a host of special considerations that do not usually arise in negotiations between purely private firms. State corporations' freedom of contract may be limited by law or regulations. They may be required to use standard-form contracts that include mandatory clauses on payment terms, insurance, and guarantees, to mention just a few. They may also be tied by the rigid rules and regulations controlling government departments. It is therefore important for an American executive to understand the laws and regulations governing the state-owned corporation represented on the other side of the table.

It is also important to understand how the state corporation relates to the government itself. For example, most state corporations are "supervised" by a particular government ministry. Thus, a national hotel corporation is supervised by a Ministry of Tourism and the national airline may be controlled by a Ministry of Transport. Are the individual corporations free to contract on their own, or must their agreements be approved by the relevant ministry to become effective? On the other hand, if the creditworthiness or reliability of the state corporation is uncertain, you may wish to secure the signature of an officer of the ministry as a guarantor or party to the deal.

If you want the government to be a party to a deal, be sure that the government representatives thoroughly understand your intent and that the contract clearly reflects that fact. In one case that has been the subject of much litigation, an investment contract for the development of a resort near the pyramids in Egypt stated that the parties to the deal were the state-owned Egyptian Hotel Corporation and a foreign company. At the closing, the president of the foreign company insisted that the minister of tourism also sign the contract on behalf of the Egyptian government. Eventually, the minister did sign, adding the words "approved, agreed, and ratified." Three years later the Egyptian government summarily canceled the contract in the face of a public outcry against building a "Disneyland" so near one of the world's most revered archaeological sites. The foreign investor sued both the hotel corporation and the Egyptian government in arbitration and won an award against both. On appeal to the courts of France, where the arbitration took place, the government successfully argued that the minister had not signed as a party to the contract, but only as the supervising authority over the hotel corporation: he was merely approving the hotel corporation's participation in the deal. The case is still in the courts.

GOVERNMENTS ARE DIFFERENT

Governments also enjoy sovereign immunity, which means that they cannot be sued in a court of law. In commercial deals, government departments or state corporations may also try to claim immunity from lawsuits. The laws of many countries take the position that a foreign government may not claim immunity for "commercial acts." So if an Indonesian government corporation refused to honor its contract to purchase rice, it could not avoid a lawsuit in the United States or in many other countries by claiming sovereign immunity. The purchase of rice is a commercial act. Some countries, however, do not recognize the commercial-act exception to the doctrine of sovereign immunity. To avoid any doubt on this question in negotiating a deal, a government or state agency should specifically agree in the contract to waive or give up its sovereign immunity should a dispute arise in connection with the transaction. Courts throughout the world recognize and enforce these explicit waivers.

Since government entities in business are usually subsidized by the state treasury, their principal goal may not be the maximization of profit, but social and economic ends. For example, if a manufacturing joint venture between a U.S. company and a foreign state-owned corporation were to be faced by a decline in demand for its products, the reaction of the U.S. partner might be to lay off workers. However, the state corporation, despite reduced profitability, might reject that solution to prevent an increase in unemployment in the country. It is important to recognize and discuss divergences of goals at the negotiating table rather than be surprised by them later on. Like Anna and the children in *The King and I*, joint-venture partners from private and public sectors should spend signif-

icant time getting to know one another before they begin to
do business.

By virtue of their government status, ministries and state
corporations often behave differently in negotiations than private companies would. Officials of government corporations
and entities often bring to the negotiating table bureaucratic
attitudes and approaches that introduce rigidity into the deal-
making process. For one thing, they resist being considered
as equals to the private businesspersons on the other side of
the table. Indeed, any suggestion that the two sides are equals
may be considered an insult. Government officials represent
their country, and a sovereign country is not the equal of a
private business, no matter how large. Any slight to a government official may be considered an affront to the dignity
of the nation.

In one instance, an African minister asked for a meeting
with the head of a mining company that had operations in his
country. The meeting took place in the office of the minister
of mines and was attended by nine other government ministers.
The minister said that the government wanted to renegotiate
its concession agreement with the company to obtain a greater
share of mine revenues, and he listed the points that needed
to be discussed. In response, the chairman of the company
reviewed each item, but at one point flatly said, "We cannot
entertain that." To emphasize his position, he struck the table
with his hand. The minister immediately adjourned the meeting
and refused to continue the discussion. While the response of
the mining company chairman might have been acceptable in
a negotiation between two private companies, it was inappro-
priate in a discussion with what amounted to nearly the entire
government of a sovereign state. Instead of an outright rebuff,
the chairman should have shown a willingness to listen and to
discuss all of the government's concerns. Such flexibility, of

course, does not mean that a company has to give in on every point. In this case, it took nearly nine months to get negotiations going again, and during that time the government made operations difficult for the company. Ultimately, the two sides did renegotiate the mining concession.

If governments have special powers and privileges in business negotiations that private companies do not, they are also at times vulnerable to pressures that companies do not usually face. For one thing, governments depend on a wide variety of supporters—political parties, labor unions, military officers, the media. Business negotiators may use these various pressure groups to influence a government's position in negotiations. When Chrysler negotiated to sell its money-losing, ineffective operations in the United Kingdom to the British government, it reacted to the government's low initial offer by threatening to liquidate its factories one by one, beginning with a plant located in an important electoral district in Scotland. The British Labour government at the time had a very slim majority and depended on Scotland for support. In the face of Chrysler's threat, Labour leaders in Scotland put strong pressure on the government to keep the plant open. In the end, the government increased its offer significantly, and made a deal with Chrysler.[1]

LAW IN THE BLACK BOX

If the political system is a black box for U.S. business executives, so is the legal system. Here one must be concerned about the impact of local law on the negotiating process as well as on the final deal that may emerge. In some countries, the very act of undertaking negotiations may create certain legal obligations. For example, under French law, beginning negotiations for a purpose other than trying to make a contract may be a civil wrong. Many legal systems impose obligations of good faith, honesty, and disclosure of pertinent information upon negotiators.

The process of negotiation involves making proposals and counterproposals. It requires putting options on the table and then considering alternatives. The parties may agree on individual points on the often unstated condition that other issues are settled. In this situation of flux, there is sometimes a danger that the local law will find that the parties had made a contract as to certain points before actually signing a formal document.

Suppose that a U.S. manufacturer, seeking to sell aircraft to a foreign government, is met with a demand that its company also buy a certain quantity of canned hams, a principal product of the foreign country. If the two sides work out satisfactory terms for the canned hams, but cannot agree on a deal for the aircraft, the U.S. manufacturer does not want to find itself obligated to buy the hams because the two contracts were clearly linked. To prevent such a result, a negotiator at the outset should make clear to the other side, preferably in writing, that no contract will come into existence unless and until the parties sign a formal document embodying their entire agreement. The letter of intent that sets the stage for detailed negotiations should normally include such a clause. This stipulation has the added benefit of facilitating a negotiating atmosphere in which the parties feel free to propose creative options without fear of being prematurely trapped into a contract. In a few cases where this precaution was not made clear, one of the parties was able to argue that they arrived at an oral contract in the negotiations and that the written contract was simply a formality, a memorandum for the record, not the essence of the contract itself.

Foreign law also directly affects the negotiation process when, in response to a proposal or request, the other side

responds flatly, "Our law doesn't permit that." In a negotiation between two Americans, that response would not go
unquestioned or unchallenged. One side would at least ask the
other for citation of chapter and article of the law in question.
When a foreign executive makes that statement in a negotiation
with an American, the American often accepts this pronounce-
ment without serious question. After all, the foreign executive
must know what he is talking about—it's his law, isn't it?
Then, too, the American usually has no basis to challenge his
counterpart on this point: he simply does not know the foreign
law.

Unquestioning acceptance of the other side's pronounce-
ments on its law is a mistake. A foreign executive is as likely
to be wrong about his or her local law as a U.S. executive is
about American law. The law in question may be capable of
more than one interpretation, and a skillful lawyer may be able
to find or develop an interpretation favoring your position. If
the other side does raise a legal objection to a proposal, you
should ask politely for a full explanation of the point and, if
possible, a copy of the law or regulation it is relying upon.
Once you fully understand its legal position, seek independent
legal advice to verify it.

LAW TALK AT THE TABLE

Much of the talk at a negotiating table involves legal words
and ideas, even if no lawyers are present. Words like "property," "company," "contract," and "debt," to name just a
few, are basic to a deal maker's vocabulary. They are legal
concepts that have meaning for a business executive by reference to a particular legal system. Different legal systems
may define these words in different ways.

An American executive encountering a foreign legal system

for the first time should be aware that the differences between U.S. laws and foreign laws are often much more fundamental than the variations among state laws in the United States. The two sides in an international negotiation often come from two different "legal traditions," so that the legal concepts, categories, and techniques each uses in thinking about a business problem are totally dissimilar. These differences may lead to misunderstandings between the parties. For example, American executives understand the difference between real property and personal property, and they use these terms in conversation all the time. In France, property is also divided into two categories: immovable and movable. This apparently similar duality sometimes leads negotiators to believe erroneously that immovable property in France is the same thing as real property in the United States. As a result, an American negotiator for the sale of a business in which all the "immovable property" is to be transferred may interpret these words as meaning "real property," thereby laying the foundation for misunderstanding. For example, French law classifies farm animals and agricultural machinery as part of a farm's immovable property, but they would not ordinarily be included within the American concept of real property.

Persons coming from different legal traditions may approach the task of making contracts differently. Certain European lawyers prefer a contract to be a statement of general principles to guide the parties' relationship. But American lawyers believe that an appropriate contract is a detailed set of rules drawn up to govern all future contingencies. Insistence on adhering to one approach over the other can sometimes create friction. The American considers the European's generalist approach as creating future uncertainties and opportunities for the other side to wiggle out of the deal. The European may view the

American's detailed approach as evidence of mistrust and a fruitless attempt to control future events.

Beyond questions of vocabulary and technique, the very notion of "law" may have different meanings in different countries. In many parts of the world, unwritten tribal, religious, or ethnic customs have the force of law. They therefore can have a direct impact on a deal you are trying to consummate.

In Africa, customary tribal law affects rights in land. Although the government may grant you a piece of land on which to build your factory, you may find that local groups hold grazing or agricultural rights on the land, which will interfere with your use. What should you do in this situation? You might ask the government to send in the military or the police to get rid of what you consider to be illegal squatters. If the government does send in the troops, you will be faced with trying to run your operation while engaging in continuing conflicts with the local people. Their position will undoubtedly be that their rights in the land predate the very existence of the government and that the government had no right to give you something it does not own. In their eyes, the government acted illegally. The other option, which is probably the far wiser alternative, is to negotiate a settlement with the local tribe or group.

The best solution of all, of course, is to identify and solve a problem *before* you sign any deal. For instance, a multinational corporation negotiated to build an agroindustrial complex in the Sudan on 100,000 acres to be granted to it by the government. Before making a contract, it hired an anthropologist to determine precisely the rights that local tribes had in that land. As a result, the corporation identified the specific groups and customary rights that might affect its future use of land, and it proceeded, with the government's help, to work out arrangements with the tribes so that traditional cattle-grazing rights would not interfere with the crops that the corporation intended to grow.

In order to penetrate the black box of foreign law and politics, a U.S. executive should follow a few basic rules.

1. Never assume that the other side's system works exactly the way yours does.
2. Do not take for granted that the words and concepts you use have exact equivalents for the other side, and do not assume that the words and concepts the other side uses fit precisely with yours.
3. To clarify legal meaning during discussion, seek to define terms and, above all, give examples of how they apply in practice.
4. For any sizable deal, obtain the help of an expert on local law.

FOREIGN LEGAL ADVICE

In most cases, you will need help to penetrate the black box of foreign law. That help will ordinarily be in the person of a lawyer or legal adviser in the country where you are trying to do business. An initial task for you or your American lawyer is to choose the right person.

The selection of a local lawyer is complicated by several factors. First, the organization and operation of the legal profession in a foreign country may be quite different from what exists in the United States. Consider Indonesia, where you would not approach a lawyer to organize a corporation, but would seek out a notary, a legally trained professional who bears no resemblance at all to the American notary public. In many countries, lawyers do not specialize in taxation. If you want tax advice, you consult an accountant. Generally, when you are looking for a local lawyer to work on a deal, you should specify precisely the kinds of tasks you want to accomplish. It sometimes happens that the best person to accomplish that task in a given country is not a "lawyer" at all. Therefore, the agroindustrial company mentioned earlier turned to an anthropologist, not a lawyer, to gain an understanding of the customary law affecting its proposed land grant in the Sudan.

A second major problem in obtaining good legal advice is that while a foreign country may have many lawyers on its rolls, few of them have the required skills to work on a big international deal. Most probably are not fluent in written and spoken English. More often than not, they have been trained primarily for courtroom work, so they have little knowledge of and experience with financial, corporate, and business matters so essential to an international business transaction. As a result, only a handful of lawyers — perhaps as few as three or four in small developing nations — handle most foreign business in some countries.

Identifying appropriate candidates can be a time-consuming process. Directories of lawyers can be of assistance in this respect, but these publications are merely a starting point, since they do not provide qualitative evaluations of the lawyers listed. The best source of guidance is a person who knows a foreign lawyer and has had an opportunity to observe that lawyer's work. American companies already doing business in a country can be of great help, and the consular section of the U.S. embassy in the country usually keeps a list of local lawyers who serve major American clients. Local businesspersons, banks, foreign lawyers in neighboring countries, and U.S. law firms with foreign offices may also provide you with useful information.

Do not select a local legal adviser without a personal interview. It is best to interview three or four candidates before making a final decision. During the interview, you want not only to determine the candidate's training, experience, English language ability, and scale of fees, but also to learn about the candidate's relationships with the host country government, knowledge of the bureaucracy, and any possible conflicts of interest. In countries where a relatively few lawyers handle virtually all foreign business, possibilities for conflicts of interest are rife, and local lawyers sometimes are not sufficiently sensitive to that issue.

You should ordinarily interview a candidate in his or her office during business hours rather than at a hotel or restaurant, as is sometimes done. In this way you can come to know the candidate's organization, support services, and facilities. It often happens that a brilliant and polished foreign lawyer does not have the typists, secretaries, library, or legal associates necessary to meet the needs of a large American company. Because foreign clients tend to give their business to a few local lawyers, the lawyers may take on a work load that they cannot handle, especially in countries where lawyers usually practice individually rather than in firms.

The Squeeze

The challenge of foreign law and politics for a U.S. business is not only to understand them but also to operate simultaneously within two or more legal and political systems. By engaging in international business, a company enters into an arena of intense legal and political pluralism. An export sale, a direct foreign investment, or a technology transfer brings you into contact with the laws and political authority of another country, but at the same time you remain subject to the laws and government authority of your own country. Legal and political pluralism means that a transaction may be taxed by two or more governments, a contract may be subject to two or more legal systems, and a dispute may be decided by courts in two different countries.

An extreme example of the kind of legal and political pluralism that a business deal may face was the construction of the Soviet trans-Siberian pipeline in the early 1980s. American companies and their European subsidiaries were squeezed between the law and political power of the United States and the law and political authority of our European allies. In that case, European subsidiaries of U.S. corporations arranged contracts to supply equipment and technology to a pipeline that the Soviets were building to carry natural gas from Siberia to Europe. The U.S. government considered the pipeline a security threat, so it ordered the European subsidiaries of American companies not to participate. Attracted by the economic benefits, the European governments demanded that those subsidiaries respect their supply contracts. Only diplomacy at the highest level between the United States and Europe finally solved the problem.

Although the Soviet pipeline case attracted considerable attention, it is certainly not a unique example of legal and political pluralism in international business. Different laws give the parties different expectations. Under U.S. law, a failing corporation can seek the protection of a bankruptcy court. Instead of being liquidated, it is given an opportunity to reorganize and continue doing business. In Australia, reorganization in bankruptcy does not exist. A failing company either makes a deal with its creditors or it liquidates. Therefore, creditors in the United States and Australia have two different sets of expectations. If they want to do business in each other's country, they must adjust those expectations.

The practice of global deal making is always a matter of complying with or avoiding a multiplicity of different countries' laws, rules, and policies, of weaving between overlapping legislation and political decisions made by several governments. The problem of the legal and political squeeze is always on the minds of international negotiators.

APPROACHES TO PLURALISM

Deal makers use a variety of techniques to cope with legal pluralism. *One technique is to agree on one set of laws to govern a deal.* In light of that, virtually all international business contracts contain a clause stating that the law of a particular country, to the exclusion of all other laws, will apply to a transaction and to any disputes that may arise between the parties. The purpose here is to assure that their agreement will be applied and interpreted in a predictable manner consistent with their original intent. Making no choice increases uncertainty. Without any specific choice of law to govern a contract, a court would usually apply the law of the country judged to have the "most significant relationship" to the deal, a concept that may lead to a variety of results. This kind of choice affects only the law governing the application and interpretation of a contract. It has no effect against regulations by governments, as in the Soviet pipeline case, taken in the public interest.

Beyond mere predictability, a particular law may be chosen because it is favorable to one of the parties or is highly developed in the area of the transaction. Or the choice may be motivated by a desire to avoid a country whose law is unclear or undeveloped. It is for these reasons that virtually all Eurodollar loans to Third World countries opt for New York governing law rather than the law of the borrower.

The selection of a particular foreign law to govern a contract may occasionally lead to conflict in certain negotiations. For example, a government, for reasons of sovereignty and national pride, is often reluctant to accept a law other than its own. On the other hand, foreign corporations are unwilling to accept that government's law because the government has the power to change that law later on and therefore affect a contract. In such cases, the parties often agree to accept "general principles of law" or "general principles of international law" as the basic rules to govern the contract in any future disputes. They usually couple this approach with the technique of writing as detailed and comprehensive a contract as possible in hopes of minimizing the need to refer to any law to interpret the contract during the life of the deal.

Another technique for avoiding the squeeze is to organize a transaction so that certain parts of it have contact with countries whose laws and policies are favorable, while scrupulously avoiding countries whose laws and policies are unfavorable. To illustrate, some countries impose tax only on income earned inside the country while others tax on a worldwide basis. The first type may be a good place to establish a corporation that will receive income from foreign investments or licensing arrangements.

Hometown Justice

For global deal makers, the final and perhaps ultimate challenge posed by the law and politics of another country is that, at some point, their company may be unfairly treated because it is foreign. This is the problem of hometown justice. Negotiators may face hometown justice either before or after the deal is made. The defensive weapons that the deal maker may use are different in each case.

THE GOVERNMENT AS GHOST NEGOTIATOR

Before a deal is made, discriminatory government action may take many forms, but the purpose is ultimately to prevent the making of a contract or to extract a better deal than usual for the government itself or for local companies. A government may order state-owned corporations, or even local private companies, not to negotiate with you. It may have laws and regulations requiring review of contracts with foreigners or even specifying terms to be included in contracts. For example, rather than allow the conditions of a foreign investment to be worked out through the give-and-take of negotiations, the local law may specify "performance requirements" for a project, perhaps a required amount of local raw materials to be used in production or a minimum amount of products that must be exported. And instead of allowing a royalty payment on a licensing agreement to be arrived at by bargaining, government regulations may fix a ceiling. Thus, the government, through the legal and regulatory system it controls, may be an unseen "ghost" negotiator at the table. For executives accustomed to a free-market economy, this kind of system tilts unfairly in favor of local companies. For the government, the system is merely a way to strengthen the inferior bargaining power of local business interests.

Faced with these challenges before a deal has even been set, what should a U.S. executive do? The first task is to learn the facts precisely. If discriminatory action has been taken because of a law or regulation, obtain a copy of that legislation and analyze it carefully. If a government has directed a local firm not to deal with you, that direction is not likely to be a matter of public record. You will then have to use indirect methods to learn of the order and why it was given. The government may have taken that action because of its relations with the United States, its relations with the country of one of your competitors, or for many other reasons. Once you understand the reason, you may be able to devise a deal that meets the government's interests and at the same time accomplishes what you want.

If you are able to establish that a foreign government is discriminating against you, one course of action is to seek the help of the U.S. government. The country concerned may have made treaties and agreements with the United States protecting U.S. companies against discrimination and guaranteeing them "most favored nation treatment," which means that American companies are not to be treated worse than businesses from other countries. The treaties may also have guaranteed U.S. companies "national treatment," which means that American companies are to receive the same treatment that the government gives to its local companies. These treaties and agreements give the United States a strong basis to press the foreign government to allow American companies the freedom to negotiate deals on the same basis as other companies. Thus, faced with an obstructionist foreign government behind the scenes, you should adopt a strategy of bringing the U.S. government into negotiations.

Whether the American government will actively work on your behalf depends on a variety of factors, including the state of U.S. relations with the host country, the existence of similar cases, and the views and background of the ambassador. The U.S. embassy will look at your problem not as a separate and distinct concern, but as one element in the entire fabric of relations between the United States and the host country. If the United States is in the process of seeking a major concession, such as the rights to build a naval base in the country, it probably will not press your concern too actively. If, on the other hand, several other U.S. companies have complained of discriminatory treatment, the embassy will probably take more vigorous action.

WHEN THE PARTY IS OVER

Deals are done with high hopes and champagne toasts. Having signed a contract, the parties to the transactions look to the future with great expectations. Yet there is always the risk that sometime after you sign the documents and begin the project the local government will intervene to change the deal, usually in its favor. The plant you have invested in is nationalized. The long-term supply contract you are relying upon is canceled. The profits you have made in local currency are no longer convertible into dollars. Your American technicians are thrown out of the country. And for some strange reason, you can't get a visa to visit the country to inspect operations. These are the political risks of a global deal.

In making any deal, the negotiator must identify the political risks and then try to structure the transaction to minimize them. As part of a foreign investment project, the U.S. investor might obtain political risk insurance against nationalization, inconvertibility of local currency, or physical destruction resulting from war, revolution, or civil disturbance. It might also obtain guarantees from the country's central bank to convert sufficient local currency into dollars to allow the project to pay its debts and distribute profits to its owners. The investor might organize the operation so that the foreign subsidiary is dependent on the parent for components, technology, and other production needs. The host government would therefore hesitate to expropriate or intervene lest the parent stop supplying these essentials and thereby make the subsidiary valueless.

Once the deal is signed, the U.S. company should also take care to maintain strong relations with the government and to assure itself a good image with the public. One useful approach is to give the project as much of a local identity as possible through the use of local managers and partners and the training of host country nationals to assume skilled positions. As one experienced international executive advised, "Nationalize yourself before they nationalize you." In a real sense, protection of a signed deal from political risks is a continuing process of negotiation between you and the foreign government concerned. The aim of that negotiation is to convince the government that its goals and yours remain identical. Troubles develop when the government comes to believe that your two goals have diverged.

These and other techniques help to lower the political risks of global deals, but they are not foolproof. In the end, a sovereign state has the power to take property, cancel contracts, and stop business activity. If those actions cost you money, the real issue is whether you simply have to bear the loss or whether the government will be forced to compensate you. A question of equal importance relates to who will make that decision. To leave the matter to the courts of the country concerned is to raise the specter of hometown justice, of biased decisions that are made to protect national interests rather than to arrive at a fair and legal result. What is needed is a neutral decision maker outside the control or influence of the foreign government concerned.

INTERNATIONAL ARBITRATION

One way to achieve a satisfactory result is for the parties to a deal to agree to submit any future disputes between them to a neutral decision maker. This, in fact, is what is done in the vast majority of international transactions. It takes the form of international commercial arbitration.

Arbitration, an age-old method of solving disputes, is found in most of the world's cultures. While it has many variations, basically it is a process whereby two persons agree to submit a present or future dispute to a third person and further agree that they will carry out that third person's decisions. Most international contracts today contain a clause that should a dispute arise between the parties (even if one of the parties is a government or state corporation), they will not go to court, but will refer the matter to an arbitrator or arbitrators, usually located in a third country, to hear the matter and make a decision. In many cases, there are three arbitrators — one chosen by each side and the third selected by the two appointed arbitrators.

In addition to assuring neutrality, arbitration avoids the uncertainty of going to court, and the further possibility that the court systems of two or more countries may become involved. Moreover, because the parties choose the arbitrators (who are to act independently, not as representatives), they have greater assurance that the arbitral tribunal will have appropriate international business expertise than if they had left the matter to the ordinary courts of law. In addition, since the proceedings are private, the parties, by using arbitration instead of the courts, can avoid unwanted publicity. Privacy may tend to protect business secrets and create an atmosphere in which a negotiated settlement might take place.

Arbitration is of two types: institutional and ad hoc. In

institutional arbitration, the parties select a specific institution to administer their arbitration proceeding. Many institutions exist around the world to handle arbitration. The best known include the International Chamber of Commerce, the American Arbitration Association, the London Court of Arbitration, the Stockholm Chamber of Commerce, and the Zurich Chamber of Commerce. Each one has its own rules and procedures. In an ad hoc arbitration, the parties administer the arbitration themselves according to rules they have agreed upon.

Institutional arbitration has several advantages. First, the institution selected has a tested set of rules and procedures to govern the arbitration. Second, it has an administrative organization to assist in managing the proceedings. Third, unless the parties agree otherwise, the arbitration institution appoints the arbitrators from its own list of experts and makes other necessary decisions to advance the arbitration. In addition, the arbitration institution, for a fee, can provide hearing rooms, secretarial services, translation facilities, and other support services. The primary disadvantage of institutional arbitration is cost. The fees charged for administering an international commercial arbitration can be substantial. Ad hoc arbitration is therefore usually cheaper, and it gives the parties the flexibility to design an arbitration mechanism that meets their particular needs.

Arbitration is not "palm tree justice." The arbitrators follow definite procedures and are required to apply the law in making their decision. Arbitration is, however, private justice. This means that the parties, not the state treasury, must finance it. Therefore, the parties have to pay not only for their lawyers, but also for the arbitrators and for the institution that they select to administer the proceedings.

Having negotiated an arbitration clause into a deal, a business executive may well ask: What will make the other side respect that clause, especially when they have already shown that they refuse to abide by other parts of our contract? And even if they do go to arbitration, what will make them accept an arbitration decision that goes against them? The answer to these two questions is to be found in a treaty, the United Nations Convention on the Recognition and Enforcement of Foreign Arbitral Awards, that has been signed by most countries, except for a number in Latin America. By this treaty, the courts of the countries that signed it must enforce arbitration agreements and arbitration awards. So, if an American company has a long-term supply contract with Nigeria that provides for arbitration in Paris, and the arbitrator makes an award in favor of the American company, that company can enforce the award in the courts of any country that has signed the treaty and in which the Nigerian government has assets.

International commercial arbitration is by no means perfect, but it is the preferred method for resolving international business disputes. It is an important element in avoiding the problem of hometown justice in global deal making.

7

Moving Money

WHEN YOU MAKE a business deal in the United States, you expect to pay or be paid in U.S. dollars. When you make a deal outside the United States, you have many more payment options. You can make a deal in Japanese yen, French francs, British pounds, Argentinean pesos, Saudi riyals, or any of the globe's many other currencies.

Unlike purely domestic deals, international business transactions take place in an arena of many different monetary systems and currencies. There is no single global money for making payment. The existence of so many currencies creates another potential barrier in international business negotiations. In making any business deal, the parties at the table not only have to decide on the price and the payment date, but they must also agree on which currency to make payment in. The decision on a specific currency can have far-reaching implications for the management and profitability of a deal.

For the global deal maker, so many different monetary systems create the problem of *moving money*, which has two dimensions. First, the relative values of the world's currencies are constantly moving—fluctuating in relation to one another. That factor creates special risks and problems in structuring a global business deal. Second, many countries' currencies are not freely convertible; consequently, the deal maker who is to be paid in nonconvertible currencies must worry constantly about ways to move the value stored in them into more usable funds. Thus, money can be either movable or immovable. This chapter considers both kinds to determine how they affect negotiations and what solutions are available to handle the problems they create.

Movable Money

The values of the world's leading currencies in relation to one another are changing constantly. These relative values are known as exchange rates. Money, like any other commodity, responds to the forces of supply and demand, unless of course governments intervene to influence the market. Supply and demand for currency depend on many factors, including inflation rates, prevailing interest rates, economic growth, and political stability in the countries concerned.

THE FOREIGN EXCHANGE RISK

For the negotiator, foreign currency in a deal creates a risk. In particular, it creates risk for the company that is to pay or be paid in that currency. Between the time an agreement is signed and the time payment is received, the value of the foreign currency in relation to that company's national or desired currency may decrease so that the company ultimately receives, after conversion, less of its own currency than it expected. Similarly, if a company has to pay in foreign currency, the value of that currency may increase so that the company has to spend more of its own money than it intended in order to buy the foreign currency necessary to make payment.

A foreign exchange risk is always present for one of the parties in an international business transaction. The longer the term of a deal, the greater the risk. In 1980 a small U.S. company found a Japanese manufacturer whose price for an important type of adhesive was far cheaper than that of any manufacturer in the United States. To lock in this low-cost supply, the U.S. company signed a long-term purchase contract with the Japanese company. In the negotiations, the Japanese insisted on payment in yen, since all their manufacturing costs were payable in their own currency. The American company agreed, therefore taking on the risks of foreign exchange fluctuations.

Having reduced its raw material costs significantly, the U.S. company began making substantial profits with its line of adhesives. At the time the deal was signed in 1979, the exchange rate between the Japanese yen and the U.S. dollar was 185 yen to $1.00. Later the U.S. company earned even more money as the exchange rate increased to over 250 yen to $1.00. In 1985, however, the relation between the yen and the dollar began to change dramatically, and by 1988 the value of the yen reached 140 to the dollar — almost double what it had been a few years previously. The result was that the U.S. company began to lose money. Although the price in yen remained constant throughout this period in accordance with the contract, the number of dollars that the U.S. company needed to buy those yen increased greatly. Facing competition from other American companies, it could not raise its dollar selling price to offset the rising yen costs of adhesives. As a result, a deal that was good in 1980 turned out to be a loser by 1988.

Had the two companies struck a deal for payment in dollars, the Japanese company would have been the one to assume the foreign exchange risk, and the U.S. company would still be making a profit. Under a dollar contract, the Japanese company would have received a decreasing number of yen from each dollar payment it received. It then would have had the problem of figuring out how to meet the demands of its workers, suppliers, and bankers, all of whom expected to be paid in yen fixed by their own contracts with the Japanese manufacturer.

COPING WITH FOREIGN EXCHANGE RISK

Because the foreign exchange risk is present in any international deal, the challenge for negotiators is to find a way to cope with it. Various techniques exist, but there are basically three choices: (1) give the risk to the other side; (2) accept the risk, but protect yourself; or (3) share the risk.

Give the Risk to the Other Side

A deal maker can simply insist on being paid in his or her home currency. This maneuver throws the foreign exchange risk on the other side. The American company might have tried this approach in its negotiations with the Japanese adhesive manufacturer. In pursuing this strategy, you need to establish an objective principle to justify allocating the risk to one side or the other. One useful principle is that the side that is better able to handle the foreign exchange risk should be the one to bear it. Thus, if you have substantial costs in a specific currency, you can argue that you should be paid in that currency, and that the other side should bear the foreign exchange risk.

Many times, however, this technique of allocating the risk to the other side is unusable, either because the other side has the bargaining power to resist it or because the transaction does not allow for it. Say an American and a Japanese company were negotiating a joint venture to establish a plant in Japan.

The American company, by the very nature of the deal, assumes a foreign exchange risk since its assets in Japan will be valued in yen and any profits will be earned in yen.

Accept the Risk, but Protect Yourself

A second technique of dealing with foreign exchange risk is to accept the risk but take special measures to protect yourself against adverse fluctuations in exchange rates. One of the simplest applications of this approach is for the party bearing the risk to estimate the "cost" of foreign exchange fluctuation likely to occur before completion of payment and build that cost into the transaction. A seller of goods who agrees to be paid in a foreign currency might increase the price of the goods to take account of expected adverse changes in exchange rates. However, that party still bears the exchange risk because the actual exchange rate change may be different from what was expected.

One of the most common approaches to protecting against the exchange risk is to shift the risk to a third party or institution not directly involved in the deal that you are trying to put together. A variety of insurance-type techniques exists to achieve this goal. One method is to make a contract to purchase currency at a specific price and date in the "forward market" or "futures market." Another is to secure a foreign currency option to buy or sell currency for a fixed price during a specified period in the future. Large businesses may use other techniques, such as establishing foreign currency accounts or purchasing foreign currency bonds. Both of these may protect you against adverse changes in rates, but they may also require you to divert working capital from more profitable uses.

A company with substantial international business can manage its risks of currency fluctuations by arranging offsetting transactions—often called exposure netting—in which the risk of loss in one transaction would be counterbalanced by a gain in another. In this way, an American company's risk stemming from an obligation to pay yen in the future might be offset by a debt in yen owed to that company and payable by another company at the same future date.

All these techniques have associated transaction costs. Sound financial advice by experts in the field is necessary to use them effectively. The purpose of this chapter is not to provide detailed instruction on their use, but merely to signal that a foreign exchange risk in global deals does exist and that the deal maker should seek advice on protecting his or her company against it.

Share the Risk

It is also possible for the parties to agree on a formula that allows both of them to share the foreign exchange risk, although not necessarily equally. They could agree that some portion of the price be paid in one currency and the remainder be paid in another currency. In addition, they might also provide for payment in a unit of account such as a special drawing right (SDR) or a European currency unit (ECU), both of which are made up of a basket of different currencies. The reason for using these units of account, rather than specific currencies, is that they are likely to maintain value and experience relatively little fluctuation since the constituent currencies are often inversely correlated. In case of major fluctuation, the increases in the value of one currency are offset by corresponding decreases in the values of the other currencies. However, the value of your company's desired single currency could still fluctuate unfavorably even in relation to SDRs and ECUs.

These methods are complicated, involve transaction costs, and do not really eliminate foreign exchange risks. In the end, one of the parties usually bears most of the risk. One way to avoid injuring one party severely in a long-term transaction is to provide that if the exchange rates rise or fall by a certain percentage, the parties will renegotiate the payment provisions. Renegotiation raises another set of problems, set forth in chapter 8.

Immovable Money

So far we have been talking about freely convertible currencies, "foreign exchange" in the language of international deal makers. However, most of the world's currencies are not freely convertible. These moneys are basically immovable.

For political and economic reasons, most governments use their powers to set exchange rates for their currencies and to restrict access to the foreign exchange market. Through a complex system of regulations known as exchange controls, governments regulate the entry to, possession in, and exit from their territories of both foreign and local currencies. A common feature of many exchange control systems is to make it a crime for any resident or company in the country to hold foreign currency. A subsidiary located in that country is therefore required to convert dollar proceeds from its foreign sales immediately into local currency and deposit them with a bank in the country. In order to obtain dollars or francs or yen to purchase foreign supplies or pay dividends, the subsidiary has to apply to the country's central bank for a foreign exchange allotment. If the bank felt the request was justified, it would convert the local currency to dollars at a fixed rate of exchange. If not, the subsidiary would have to find another way to finance the purchase or simply do without.

As a result of exchange controls and government regulations, a company's ability to pay for imported raw materials, to service foreign debt, to transfer profits, or to repatriate capital depends on the host country's willingness to make foreign exchange available. In such countries, a company's bank account may be stuffed with its profits in local currency, but the business may fail unless the government is willing to let the company move its money into another, more readily usable currency. The great challenge for the international deal maker working in exchange control countries is to find mechanisms to assure adequate, freely convertible currency, also known as foreign exchange or, more simply, hard money. If it is true, as former House Speaker Thomas ("Tip") O'Neill remarked, that "money is the mother's milk of politics," it is equally true that foreign exchange is the mother's milk of global business.

MOVING THE IMMOVABLE

How, then, should deal makers go about trying to move immovable money? First, you have to recognize the problem. This means that you need to understand the exchange control system in a country and how it applies to your deal. To do that, you must not only read the regulations, but you must also talk to people who have had experience with them. At the same time, you must also recognize that exchange controls are not static. A government can change them rapidly, sometimes retroactively. So a transaction that would get you a foreign currency allotment from the central bank one day may be prohibited the next.

Second, the structure of a transaction may affect your ability to secure foreign exchange. For example, royalty payments on technology agreements may have a higher priority at a central bank than dividend payments. It may therefore be prudent to structure your relationship with that country as a technology transfer rather than as an equity joint venture. If it is an equity joint venture, you may need to include a technology transfer agreement, with substantial royalty payments, as part of the project package. In this way, you will withdraw your profits from the venture as royalties rather than dividends. Some parent companies inflate prices on the sale of raw materials and components to their foreign subsidiaries as a way to repatriate profits and evade exchange controls against payment of dividends.

A third technique is to negotiate special exemptions and privileges with a country's monetary authorities. One way is to secure central bank guarantees of hard currency for specific types of payments to be made by the project. The willingness of the bank to do this will depend on the project's importance to the local economy. If the project will have earnings in foreign currency, you might secure permission to hold those earnings offshore in foreign exchange bank accounts rather than depositing them with the host country central bank.

A fourth approach is to seek a guarantee or assurance of hard currency availability from a sound financial institution outside the country in question. On a foreign investment project, you might obtain political risk insurance, from either public or private sources, on the convertibility of profits. And in connection with a long-term commodity purchase agreement, you might require the other side to obtain a letter of credit confirmed by a bank in the United States.

Finally, if all else fails in your effort to avoid exchange controls and obtain foreign exchange, you might turn to an age-old practice that businesses have used when dealing with organizations that are strapped for cash: take it out in trade.

TAKING IT OUT IN TRADE

Countries with limited foreign exchange often seek to obtain the goods and technology they need through bartering arrangements known as countertrade. Once primarily used in deals with the Soviet Union and Eastern Europe, countertrade has spread to most of the Third World and even beyond. Today it accounts for between a quarter and a third of international commerce.

Countertrade covers a wide range of countries, products, and transactions. In 1984 Saudi Arabia purchased ten Boeing 747s and fifty Rolls-Royce engines for thirty-five million barrels of oil. A few years earlier McDonnell Douglas sold jet aircraft to Romania for, among other things, a large quantity of canned hams, which, it is said, McDonnell employees may have eaten in the company cafeteria for a long time afterward. According to one estimate, over ninety countries require some form of countertrade from foreign companies doing business with them. Therefore, executives must understand this form of global deal.

Countries engage in countertrade for many reasons, but the primary one is their lack of hard currency. They see countertrade as a way to preserve their already scarce foreign exchange holdings and still import needed goods and technology. Second, faced with increasing protectionism in foreign markets, some countries believe that countertrade allows them to escape protectionist measures. Third, as a result of development efforts and investment, many countries have increased their industrial capacity. Consequently, they have a surplus of goods (often of poor quality) that cannot be absorbed locally or sold internationally. Countertrade, they think, is a way to unload those goods. Fourth, even if a country does make products of good quality, it may not have the marketing expertise and links to sell them abroad. Countertrade, it is hoped, will allow them to use the expertise and connections of multinational corporations. Finally, for some countries countertrade is a way to avoid existing international trade commitments on pricing and quotas. For example, a barter deal for oil may allow a petroleum-producing country to avoid minimum prices established by OPEC.

Countertrade takes many forms and is called by many names. Each deal is tailored to particular circumstances. Nonetheless, one can group countertrade transactions into the following basic categories.

Barter

Pure barter is, of course, the most ancient form of international trade. It is essentially an exchange of one type of goods for another type of goods. In the modern world, pure barter takes up a relatively small proportion of countertrade, primarily because of the difficulty in matching precisely the available goods and desired needs of two parties. A trading company is often brought into more complex barter arrangements to facilitate sale of the goods, as when a small U.S. company wanted to sell enamel blackboards to the Soviet Ministry of Education and was paid in bales of used paper from schools throughout the Soviet Union. The U.S. company then turned to a European trading company to sell the paper to recycling companies in several countries.

Counterpurchase

Probably the most common form of countertrade, counterpurchase, sometimes called parallel barter, is an arrangement whereby a company contracts to sell goods or technology to a foreign purchaser for hard currency, but at the same time makes a commitment to buy (also for hard currency) goods produced in the importing country. Structurally, the difference between barter and countertrade is that barter consists of a single contract, while counterpurchase consists of two separate contracts that are linked, usually through a protocol or master agreement.

Offset

A variation of counterpurchase, offset is an arrangement through which a supplier of manufactured goods agrees to purchase certain components or services from an importing purchaser for use in making the final product to be imported. This type of countertrade has long been an element in the sale of defense systems and aircraft to foreign countries: as part of a major purchase of planes, Saudi Arabia required Boeing to invest a portion of its profits in Saudi companies.

Compensation

Sometimes called buyback, compensation is often used to finance the sale of capital goods and equipment. A purchaser acquires machinery immediately and pays the seller of the machinery in goods produced by that machinery over a period of years. The manufacturer of tire-making equipment would sell it to a foreign country and make a long-term contract to purchase a specific amount of tires produced by the equipment during a fixed period of time.

Countertrade is costly and inefficient. Arranging a deal is time-consuming, and the goods received may be difficult to sell, except at a deep discount. Western companies usually translate these risks and costs into higher prices for the goods, services, and technology they sell. Nonetheless, they have entered into countertrade deals in order to close sales that would otherwise be lost. Through their laws and policies, some countries require a portion of countertrade to be made on all major imports. In a few cases, firms have used countertrade as a way to assure a continuing long-term supply of raw materials, components, or finished products, particularly if the arrangement is linked to a firm's investment in the country.

NEGOTIATING A COUNTERTRADE DEAL

Negotiating a countertrade is a complex process that involves many issues. The first and most basic problem is to determine whether the foreign government or company you are dealing with will try to make you accept a countertrade obligation. One tactic that developing countries sometimes use is to negotiate a deal as if it were for cash and then announce in the final stages that they expect you to sign a countertrade contract as well. This maneuver places you in a difficult situation, since obviously your cash price and your countertrade price for goods will differ because of the added costs that a countertrade transaction involves. One way to avoid this tactic is to make sure before specifying the sale price that the other side will not require countertrade as part of the deal.

If a country does require countertrade, determine the precise nature and scope of that obligation. The countertrade obligation is usually stated in terms of a "compensation ratio," which is the percentage of the value of the export that will be subject to counterpurchase. Government directives on this point are usually secret. Negotiators from a developing country often begin by demanding a very high ratio—from 50 percent to 100 percent—but may ultimately settle for as little as 25 percent. Numerous factors may influence their final position on the ratio, including the state of the country's foreign currency reserves and the importance of the goods to the country's development plans.

The nature of the countertrade goods, their price, and their quality are also negotiated issues in putting together a countertrade deal. Sometimes the exact goods to be purchased are not specified at the time the contract is signed. Rather, the party with the countertrade obligation is to select them from lists to be supplied later by the country's foreign trade organization. When the lists are presented, they may be out of date and the goods no longer available. And usually the goods offered are exactly the ones that the country cannot sell for cash because of their poor quality.

Because most companies with a countertrade obligation want to choose goods from as wide a range as possible, the extent of that range may also be the subject of negotiation. Sometimes the countertrading party may be limited only to those goods produced by the company that is buying its products. Many countries widen the scope of selection to merchandise produced or marketed by any of their foreign trade organizations.

In planning its negotiating strategy, a U.S. company should decide precisely to what extent it is willing to make a countertrade commitment and specifically the kinds of products it is willing to accept. These goods may be divided into various categories:

1. Products that can be used in the company's own operations, such as components
2. Raw materials, particularly if they are marketable at established world prices through known channels
3. Goods that relate to the company's own product lines

and therefore can be sold through its own marketing organization

4. Manufactured products unrelated to the company's operation

Negotiators generally find this last group of goods to be least desirable because they pose the greatest risks of unprofitable resale. The goods must either be assigned to a trading house for disposal or marketed at a discount to a third party, with all the related costs. Obviously, within the category of manufactured goods, those which require no after-sale service are the most preferable.

Since countertrade goods are usually not determined at the time a contract is made, the specification of a price for the goods can create problems. The seller may also be tempted to overreach. To deal with this problem in a buyback arrangement involving agricultural goods or raw materials, the price may be set according to a recognized index or some other formula. In cases of finished or semifinished goods, the contract may call for periodic price readjustments. One formula often used provides that the price of the goods shall be the "acceptable international price at the time of purchase." Another protective mechanism is a most-favored-customer clause.

A company usually prefers as long a period as possible to make its countertrade purchases so as to have enough time to locate customers and reduce storage and other associated costs. A developing country usually insists upon a penalty provision if the firm fails to fulfill its countertrade obligation. The penalty, most often stated as a percentage of the unfulfilled part of the obligation, may range from 10 percent to 15 percent. A guarantee or standby letter of credit may be required as security for this penalty.

Finally, a countertrade arrangement should allow a firm to assign its countertrade obligations to a trading company that will take over the goods and dispose of them through its own channels.

A TACTIC TO ACCOMPLISH DEALS

The U.S. government has criticized countertrade as costly, inefficient, discriminatory, a burden on international commerce, and a blow to the multilateral trading system. All that may be true. Nevertheless, with all its complex variations, this technique of structuring a transaction as goods for goods rather than goods for money is effective for overcoming monetary barriers in international business. For negotiators, it is a way to complete deals that might otherwise never happen.

8

Renegotiating Deals

A DEAL is a prediction. A negotiation is always about the future. The parties to a deal use their contract and its enforcement mechanisms to assure that specified acts will take place in the days, weeks, months, and years ahead. An American electrical equipment manufacturer will deliver a promised generator to Bangladesh in six months' time. A Brazilian borrower will repay its loan to a New York bank in five years. A French mining company with a concession in Nigeria will be able to take minerals out of the country over the next half century.

Change, of course, is the one constant in life. Changes in circumstances happen all the time in both domestic and international business. Deal makers' predictions at a negotiating table inevitably have to confront the realities of change later on. This chapter first considers how deal makers should negotiate to reduce the adverse risks of change, then what they should do when fundamental change strikes a deal.

The risk of change in the international arena seems far greater than in purely U.S. business settings. War, revolution, closed trade routes, currency devaluations, nationalizations, and sudden changes in governments are just a few of the types of events that have severe and widespread consequences for any international deal. Specific examples within the past two decades include Iraq's invasion of Kuwait, the closing of the

Suez Canal during the 1973 October War, the Latin-American debt crisis, the fall of the Shah of Iran, and coups in much of Africa. As a result of such events, the American equipment manufacturer may find its generators stuck in the Suez Canal for months, the Brazilian debtor may have no foreign exchange to repay its debts, and the French mine developer may have its concession nationalized.

Experienced deal makers know that the challenge of international business negotiations is not just "getting to yes," but also staying there. International business agreements, solemnly signed and sealed after hard bargaining, often break down because of changes in circumstances or attitudes of the parties. When a change in circumstances means that the cost of respecting a contract for one of the parties is greater than the cost of abandoning it, the result is usually rejection or renegotiation. The two sides either walk away from each other for good or walk back to the negotiating table to restructure their deal. A traditional theme in international business circles is the lament over the "unstable contract," the profitable agreement that the other side refuses to respect. Instability and sudden change, then, are the final barriers to global deal making.

The Causes of Instability

Although hard evidence on the subject is lacking, anecdotal information suggests that contractual instability is more prevalent in international business than in a purely domestic setting. Certainly one can say that international business transactions involve special factors not present in domestic business deals and that these factors heighten the risk of contractual instability. First, because the international environment itself is so unstable, international business dealings seem particularly susceptible to sudden changes such as currency devaluations, coups, wars, and radical shifts in governments and government policies.

Second, mechanisms for enforcing agreements are often less sure or more costly in the international arena than in the domestic setting. If the other side does not have effective access to the courts to enforce a contract or to seize assets, a party to a burdensome contract may feel it has little to lose in rejecting a contract or demanding renegotiation with an expressed or implied threat of outright repudiation.

Third, as shown in chapter 6, foreign governments and government corporations are often important participants in international business dealings. They often reserve to themselves the right to repudiate burdensome contracts on grounds of protecting national sovereignty and public welfare.

Finally, the world's diverse cultures and legal systems attach differing degrees of binding force to a signed contract and recognize varying causes to justify avoidance of onerous obligations. For example, an American company in a transaction with a Japanese firm may view their signed contract as the essence of the deal and the source of rules governing their relationship in its entirety. The Japanese, however, see the deal as a partnership that is subject to reasonable changes over time, a partnership in which one party ought not to take unfair advantage of purely fortuitous events like radical and unexpected movements in exchange rates or the price of raw materials. Ironically, as a result of the rise in the value of the Japanese yen, certain American companies, tied to long-term supply agreements payable in yen for components and materials produced in Japan, relied upon this distinctly un-American approach to contracts to seek renegotiation of payment terms that unanticipated monetary changes had made unprofitable.

Rejection and Renegotiation

When one side feels that it is tied to a contract that has become unfair or unreasonable on account of changed circumstances, it usually attempts renegotiation before outright rejection. We have seen attempts to redo many existing deals. Since the outbreak of the international debt crisis in 1982, Western commercial banks and their Third World borrowers have been engaged in a constant process of renegotiating loans that developing countries have been unable to repay, an exercise commonly known as debt rescheduling. The dramatic fall in the price of oil and gas from the heights of the early 1980s forced purchasers in the mid-1980s to try to renegotiate long-term supply agreements that once seemed profitable but had become ruinous. And the rapid decline in the value of the dollar, particularly against the Japanese yen, has since 1986 prompted attempts to renegotiate other long-term deals payable in Japanese yen.

Renegotiation in international business is by no means peculiar to the 1980s. For decades, host country governments, often with the threat of nationalization in the background, have periodically sought to revise investment arrangements that they had previously made with foreign corporations but later judged disadvantageous.

As the number and length of long-term global deals expand, executives must devote increasing attention to coping with the risk of contractual instability and renegotiation. They must seek ways to reduce the risk at the time they make the original deal, and they have to engage effectively in renegotiation if and when that risk arises. The process of renegotiation raises special problems not ordinarily encountered in negotiating the original deal. Appropriate techniques and approaches differ from those used in ordinary international deal making.

THREE TYPES OF RENEGOTIATION

To handle the problem, deal makers must understand precisely the kind of renegotiation that they are facing. The term "renegotiation" covers three fundamentally different situations, and it is important to distinguish each of them at the outset. Each raises different problems and demands different solutions. The situations are (1) post-deal, (2) intra-deal, and (3) extra-deal renegotiations.

Post-deal Renegotiations

In this situation, negotiations take place at the expiration of a contract, when the two sides, though legally free to go their own ways, nonetheless try to renew their relationship. For example, at the end of a five-year distribution contract between a U.S. manufacturer and its foreign distributor, the parties may discuss a second distribution contract, thereby "renegotiating" their original relationship. Here the renegotiation process may be very much like the negotiation of their original deal, but there are also some notable differences.

First, the manufacturer and the distributor have a shared experience of working together and a knowledge of each other's goals, methods, intentions, and reliability. Obviously, the nature of that earlier experience will significantly affect the renegotiation. The problems of cross-cultural communication that may have complicated the first negotiation will probably be far less important in the second, since the parties should have learned a great deal about each other's culture during the previous five years. Second, many of the original questions about their venture—its risks and its opportunities—have been answered, and bargaining positions in the renegotiation will certainly be shaped by that information. For instance, if the distribution company found that service on the products sold was more costly than originally contemplated, it will almost certainly demand additional service support from the manufacturer.

Finally, the willingness of the participants to reach agreement is influenced by their tangible and intangible investments in their first relationship and the extent to which those investments may be used advantageously in their second contract. The foreign distributor will have trained its employees and organized itself to handle the U.S. manufacturer's products. It may therefore prefer to negotiate a new agreement with the manufacturer rather than enter into a contract with another producer, since that would require significant new training and organizational costs. Similarly, the U.S. manufacturer, having helped to develop the marketing organization and networks of the distributor, would prefer to avoid incurring the added costs required to identify and train a new distributor.

In general, the success of post-deal renegotiations depends on the strength of the relationship built by the two sides during the original contract. If that relationship is strong, the atmosphere at the table will be one of two partners trying to solve a problem. If the relationship is weak, the prevailing mood will be that of two cautious adversaries who know each other only too well.

Intra-deal Renegotiations

A second type of renegotiation occurs when an agreement provides that, during its life at specified times, the two sides may renegotiate or at least review certain provisions. Here, renegotiation is anticipated as a legitimate activity in which both parties are to engage in good faith. In a long-term supply contract, the two sides may agree to meet periodically to determine raw material prices. Rather than leave the matter entirely open to bargaining by the parties, the contract may put limits on renegotiation by specifying a formula or criteria to be used in setting new terms. In this case, the renegotiation will focus on the interpretation and application of the formula.

Because of the length of many international deals and the wide variety of changing circumstances that may affect them, providing in the contract for some sort of periodic, intra-deal renegotiation of key elements would appear to be a wise basis for establishing a long-term relationship. In fact, these provisions are relatively rare. Many Western executives view them with suspicion and consider that such provisions increase uncertainty in an already risky type of arrangement. Moreover, they offend Western concepts of the sanctity of a contract and the need for certainty and predictability in business transactions. There is always the danger that one of the parties will use a renegotiation clause as a lever to force changes in terms that strictly speaking are not open to revision. On the other hand, some parties, such as many government officials in developing nations, consider provisions for renegotiation only at specified intervals as overly restrictive, particularly if they believe that review of contractual terms, whenever necessary, is an inherent condition of their bargain.

In countries where a deal is considered to be a relationship rather than just a contract, a provision for intra-deal renegotiation makes explicit what the nationals consider to be an implicit principle: in times of change, partners should meet to decide how to cope with that change. An intra-deal renegotiation clause, then, gives stability to an arrangement whose long-term nature creates a high risk of instability.

Extra-deal Renegotiations

The most difficult and emotional renegotiations are those undertaken in apparent violation of an agreement, or at least in the absence of a specific clause for redoing the deal. These renegotiations take place "extra-deal," for they occur outside the framework of the existing agreement. Discussions to re-schedule Third World loans, revise petroleum prices, and re-view mineral concessions all fit within the category of extra-deal renegotiations. In each case, one of the participants is seeking relief from a legally binding obligation without any basis for renegotiation in the agreement itself.

Unlike negotiations for the original deal, which are generally fueled by both sides' hopes for future profits, extra-deal re-negotiations begin with both parties' shattered expectations. One side has failed to make the profit expected from the trans-action, and the other is being asked to give up something that it bargained hard for and expected to enjoy for a long time. And whereas both parties to a proposed new venture participate willingly, if not eagerly, in negotiations, one party always participates reluctantly, if not downright unwillingly, in an extra-deal renegotiation.

Beyond mere disillusionment, extra-deal renegotiations, by their very nature, can create bad feeling and mistrust. One side believes it is being asked to give up something to which it has a legal and moral right. It views the other side as having gone back on its word, as having acted in bad faith by reneging on the deal. Indeed, the reluctant party may even feel it is being coerced into participating in extra-deal renegotiations, since a refusal to do so would result in losing the investment it has already made in the transaction or joint venture. Thus, it is very difficult for the parties to see extra-deal renegotiations as anything more than a process in which one side wins and the other side loses.

The extra-deal renegotiations of an established arrangement may also have significant implications beyond the transaction in question. The side being asked to relinquish a contractual right may feel the need to show other companies that it is not weak, that it cannot be taken advantage of. Yielding to a demand for the renegotiation of one contract may encourage other parties to ask for renegotiation of their agreements as well. This concern for the potential ripple effect from renegotiations clearly contributed to the reluctance of international commercial banks to give in to demands by individual developing countries for a revision of loan terms. Concessions to Mexico would inevitably lead Argentina to demand equal treatment in its own renegotiation.

The desire to protect one's image and other contracts may lead a party to take a position, at least at the outset, of rejecting all changes in a relationship, no matter how small or inexpensive. Similarly, the side seeking relief from an agreement that is no longer reasonable may rely on higher political principles, such as national sovereignty or the public welfare, in order to prevail. As a result, the national governments of the parties may intervene in the process, and various types of legal actions may be threatened or actually invoked. The political dimensions of renegotiations have been present particularly in renegotiations between developing country governments and foreign corporations, as in those concerning international loans and mineral concessions.

JUSTIFYING EXTRA-DEAL RENEGOTIATIONS

Respect for agreements is a basic norm in virtually every culture. How, then, can an attempt to renegotiate a valid contract be anything more than an unprincipled power play? After all, a deal is a deal, isn't it?

Respect for agreements is indeed the rule in virtually all societies. It may even rise to the level of a universal principle of law. But in exceptional circumstances most cultures also provide relief, in varying degrees, from the binding force of a contract. "A deal is a deal" certainly expresses a fundamental rule of human relations, but so does the statement "Things have changed." In international business, the principle of changed circumstances underlies demands for renegotiation. The nature of the change in circumstances is broadly and variously interpreted, and that is the source of conflict. While a request for extra-deal renegotiations may provoke bad feeling in one party, an outright refusal to renegotiate may also create ill will on the other side since it is seen as an attempt to force adherence to a bargain that has become unreasonable.

Ultimately, the basic conflict between the parties in an extra-deal renegotiation is over the type of changed circumstances justifying extra-deal renegotiations. These circumstances may cover a broad spectrum. They range from sudden changes in objective conditions over which neither of the parties has control (such as rising exchange rates or closed trade routes) to conditions determined subjectively by one side alone (insufficient share of mineral revenues). With regard to the latter example, host country governments often reassess their relations with foreign investors on the basis of their countries' current need for foreign capital and technology. At the time the investment is first offered, the host country may believe it has no other options to secure the capital and technology needed for development than to give the investor extremely favorable terms. Later, after the capital and technology have been transferred and local entrepreneurs develop their own manufacturing capability, the government may ask to renegotiate the original agreement on the grounds that the country's economic circumstances and developmental needs have changed. The fact that the investor cannot easily remove its investment reduces the costs to the host country of demanding renegotiation.

The demand for extra-deal renegotiation can take a particularly virulent form if the disappointed party believes that the other side caused or knew about the changing circumstances. For example, if one side knew that certain events would make raw material prices increase but did not share that information at the negotiating table, the unhappy party would no doubt demand renegotiation on the grounds that it had been taken advantage of.

Approaches to Renegotiation

The side trying to redo a deal can choose various approaches to renegotiation. The first and ostensibly least offensive tactic is to cast extra-deal renegotiations as merely an effort to clarify ambiguities in an existing agreement rather than change its basic principles. This approach, at least nominally, respects the sanctity of the contract. It may therefore avoid the friction and hostility created by demanding outright extra-deal renegotiations. Perhaps a host country government grants a foreign investment project exemption from "all taxes and duties." Finding that the project is placing increasing demands on the economy, the government requires the investor to pay "user fees" for certain government services, on the grounds that they are not taxes or duties. Specifically, the government demands annual payments for police protection, road maintenance, and port administration. Through this approach, the government hopes to increase its revenue from the project while respecting its contract with the investor.

A second approach to renegotiation is to ask for reinterpretation of certain key terms owing to changes in circumstances, while still preserving the principles negotiated in the original agreement. Even if an investment project is specifically exempt from user fees under its contract, requiring it to pay the additional costs incurred by the government to supply power during an energy crisis might be a principled basis for redefining the scope of the exemption without altering the fundamental principle agreed on by the parties.

Waiver is yet a third approach that respects the sanctity of the agreement yet enables the burdened party to obtain relief. For example, a manufacturer in a distribution agreement may prefer to waive the specified sales quota required of a foreign distributor during periods of slack product demand rather than renegotiate and change the amount of the quota permanently. On the other hand, regular and continuous waivers of a contractual provision can over time be interpreted as a change in the provision itself. So the side waiving a requirement in a specific situation must make clear the exact extent and implications of its waiver.

In many cases, of course, the two sides have no choice but to face the necessity of rewriting their deal by entering into active and acknowledged extra-deal renegotiations to change the rules of their relationship. These are precisely the situations that create sharp conflict between the sanctity of a contract and the need to adapt the existing relationship to changing circumstances. What approaches are available to the reluctant side in this situation?

One approach is to put up maximum resistance and use delaying tactics in hopes of getting as good a deal as possible. Another approach is to take the initiative and propose creative options that expand or add to the original deal. In one renegotiation over oil exploration concessions in Zaire, a foreign oil company agreed to change the terms of the concession in return for a long-term contract to supply jet fuel to the country's national airline. In West Africa, a U.S. mining company took advantage of the host government's demand for an increased share of mine revenues to request that the government's right under the contract to purchase a minority interest be postponed for another ten years.

Early Negotiation to Prevent Late Change

If the risk of change and uncertainty is constant in international business, how should deal makers cope with it? They should approach the problem of renegotiation *before*, rather than after, they make their original deal. Both sides should recognize at the outset that the risk of changed circumstances is high in any long-term relationship and that at some time in the future either side may seek to reject or renegotiate the agreement.

Most modern contracts deny the possibility of change. They therefore rarely provide for adjustments to meet changing circumstances. This assumption of contractual stability has proven false time and time again. For example, most mineral development contracts assume that the agreement will last for periods of from fifteen to ninety-nine years, but they rarely remain unchanged for more than a few years. A bargain, once struck, inevitably becomes obsolete. Issues, once agreed upon, are eventually reopened later on as circumstances change.

A DEAL IS NOT FOREVER

While praising the sanctity of contract, every experienced negotiator knows that no deal is forever. Accordingly, before you arrive at the negotiating table, calculate the risks of change in any eventual deal and take account of them in developing your negotiating plans and strategies. Throughout the negotiations, remember the following principle: when the costs to the other side of rejecting a deal are less than respecting it, the risk of repudiation and renegotiation increases.[1] Your basic strategy to give stability to your deal is to assure that the other side derives sufficient benefits from keeping the agreement or incurs sufficient costs from breaking it.

To apply this strategy for a stable agreement, a deal maker should follow all three of the following steps.

Lock Them In

The first step is to embody the deal in a carefully written agreement with detailed provisions and guarantees to ensure respect for the contract to the maximum extent possible. This means that you should try to anticipate possible changes in circumstances and provide for them in the contract. At the same time, you should calculate the realistic possibility of extra-deal renegotiations and include that calculation in your plans. Consequently, prices, rates of return, and other essential terms should reflect a hard-headed assessment of the actual duration of the initial agreement, rather than the duration stated in the contract document.

The other side should fully understand the contract, particularly its inherent risks. If you try to hide those risks, you inevitably open yourself to charges of bad faith and demands for renegotiation later on. The agreement itself should identify those risks and clearly allocate them to one or both sides. International contracts often include a force majeure clause, a provision that suspends or excuses performance of specified contractual obligations on the occurrence of stated events like war, strikes, or civil unrest.

The wise deal maker should build into an agreement mechanisms to reduce the likelihood of rejection and renegotiation. The thrust of these mechanisms is either to raise the cost to the other side for not respecting the deal or, alternatively, compensate the side that has lost the benefit of the deal it made. Two common mechanisms are a performance bond and linkage.[2]

Under a performance bond, the other side or some reliable third party puts up money or property that will be turned over to one side if the other fails to perform under the contract. In a large sale of equipment, both the manufacturer and the buyer might be required to have their banks issue letters of credit. The purpose of the buyer's letter of credit is to guarantee payment to the manufacturer. The purpose of the manufacturer's letter of credit is to guarantee performance — or at least compensation for the failure to perform — if the manufacturer does not deliver equipment as promised.

Linkage, a second technique that gives stability to a contract by increasing the costs of noncompliance, can take many forms. The approach here is to link any future failure to perform a contract to adverse consequences from other parties or other relationships. The basic idea behind linkage is that those consequences increase the cost of rejection and therefore inhibit the other side from breaking its contract. A foreign investor may involve corporations and banks from many countries in an investment project on the theory that the host country might risk a conflict with one foreign company, but it would not do so with several.

Balance the Deal

Wise negotiators know that the best deal is one that is good for both sides. The second important step to a stable contract is to create a balanced agreement in the first place. If the agreement is mutually beneficial, both sides have an incentive to maintain it. Neither side will consider rejection or repudiation as an attractive alternative. A balanced agreement might be one that allocates specific risks in a venture to the party best able to bear that risk, rather than merely on the basis of raw bargaining power. It might also provide that unexpected windfalls or losses be shared by both parties, rather than accrue to one side or the other.

Control the Renegotiation

The third step to a stable contract is to provide specifically in the agreement for intra-deal renegotiations at defined intervals on specific issues that are particularly susceptible to changing circumstances. A variation of this approach is to provide for a series of linked short-term contracts that together will extend over the life of the contemplated business relationship. Each of the specific agreements will be negotiated as the relationship evolves.

Rather than dismiss the possibility of renegotiation and then be forced to consider review of the entire contract at a later time, it is better to recognize the possibility of renegotiation at the outset and set down a clear framework with which to conduct the process. In short, recognize the possibility of redoing the deal, but control the process.

Seeing Around the Corner

Making global deals in this rapidly changing world quite literally requires executives to be able to see around the corner — to anticipate future trends and forces that may have an impact on their deals. To a significant extent, those trends and forces are political in nature. They stem from government decisions and policies that affect their own countries and their relations with other nations. Although the techniques suggested in this chapter may be useful in giving stability to international deals, they are no substitute for a deal maker's own careful and constant study of international politics.

9

Paddling the Same Canoe

NEGOTIATION, if it's done right, is a process — a progressive movement toward a goal. In an international business negotiation, that goal is a deal. The job of negotiators on both sides of the table is to manage the negotiation process over obstacles and around barriers to reach the goal.

Deal makers must pursue their own companies' interests vigorously, but they also have to work together to overcome hurdles on the way to a deal. At times the two sides at the negotiating table are like two persons in a canoe who must combine their skills and strength if they are to make headway against powerful currents, through dangerous rapids, around hidden rocks, and over rough portages. Alone, they can make no progress and will probably lose control. Unless they cooperate, they risk wrecking or overturning the canoe on the obstacles in the river. Similarly, unless global deal makers find ways of working together, their negotiations will founder on the many barriers encountered in putting together an international business transaction.

The problem for deal makers from different countries is to find a way to paddle the same canoe toward a common goal. Just as canoeists need a few basic rules to propel their canoe, so deal makers should follow a few basic principles to enable them to work together to advance the negotiating process. The following ten simple rules are designed to help you and those across the table to be sure that you are paddling the same canoe in the same direction.

1. Prepare Thoroughly

Prepare thoroughly for every negotiation. You should not only understand the substance of the transaction, you should exhaustively research the countries, organizations, persons, cultures, and ideologies involved in the deal. Consult Appendix A, the Global Deal Negotiation Checklist, for help with your preparations.

2. Know Your Bottom Line

Carefully determine what you want from a deal before you start negotiations. Identify in advance precisely at what point an agreement is not in your interest compared to your other options. Beware of changing objectives in the heat of deal making.

3. Have Patience

Negotiating an international transaction is a time-consuming process, one that invariably takes longer than you originally plan. If you are not prepared to commit the time, don't get into the negotiation. Shortcuts usually fail. Establish deadlines with care and avoid ultimatums.

4. Be Perceptive

Successful negotiation requires keen perception of yourself as well as the other side. Throughout the discussions, remember the negotiator's three cameras. You must constantly and simultaneously focus on (a) your own words and actions; (b) the meaning the other side gives to your words and actions; and (c) the words and actions of the other side.

5. Show Respect

International negotiations bring you into contact with many cultures, governments, ideologies, customs, values, and beliefs. Approach each of them with respect and willingness to learn. Negotiation is fundamentally a learning process. One of the marks of inexperienced negotiators is the attitude that they have little to learn at the table. That attitude is not only perceived as arrogance by the other side, but it also prevents executives from getting the information they require to make a good deal.

Above all, do not make unfavorable comments and comparisons on the culture, ideology, and political system of the other side. Jokes on the same subjects, no matter how well intended, almost always backfire on the person who tells them. Every country has its own formalities and procedures. Learn them and respect them.

6. Be Flexible

While you should know your bottom line, you should also realize that there are many ways to arrive at it. Remain open to new approaches and search for creative solutions to allow both sides to advance their interests.

7. Form Relationships

Try to get to know the other team as individuals and develop a personal relationship with them. Socializing with them away from the table can lead to important opportunities for facilitating deal making. Showing a sincere interest in the members of the other team, their culture, and their country will give you a basis for developing a relationship. At the same time, just because they may talk, dress, and act like you, do not assume that they are like you in all respects.

8. Search for the Other Side's Needs and Interests

Throughout the negotiations, delve behind stated positions to understand the other side's real needs and interests. In the search for interests, the question is the deal maker's most powerful tool. Use it to learn as much as possible about the other side. At the same time, do not accept the other side's statements literally. Rephrase their statements in two or three ways to understand their meaning. Try to interpret their words and actions against your knowledge of the country's culture, history, ideology, and political system.

9. Accentuate the Positive

Throughout your discussions with the other side, emphasize the positive aspects of the deal and the relationship. Stress the points of agreement with your counterparts and the progress you are making in the talks. Try to make negative points in a positive way.

10. Keep Your Cool

Never become emotional at the negotiating table. Emotions cloud judgment and interfere with perception. Equally important, different cultures interpret displays of emotion differently. An angry statement that might be tolerated in negotiations in the United States may be taken as evidence of insanity in Thailand. In such a setting, your outburst may entirely destroy your credibility with the other side. As a group, skilled international negotiators are capable of great personal warmth, but the very best avoid becoming emotionally involved in making global deals.

These ten rules may appear to be simple. But then, so does paddling a canoe—until you get into the boat. They are ground rules for making global deals. If you can apply them along with your knowledge of the barriers to global deal making, you will be in a position to take advantage of the vast new business opportunities that await you beyond your borders.

Appendix A

Global Deal Negotiation Checklist

Use this checklist as a guide to preparing for and conducting your negotiations.

I. PRENEGOTIATION AND PREPARATION
  A. *Goals*
    1. What are our goals and interests in this negotiation?
       Our maximum objectives?
       Our minimum objectives?
    2. At what point is it preferable not to make a deal? What is our walk-away point?
    3. What are the goals and interests of the other side? At what point do we think they will walk away?
    4. What is our relationship and history with the other side? How will that relationship affect the discussions?
    5. Who are our competitors for this deal?
    6. What advantages do we have over our competitors?
    7. What advantages do our competitors have over us?
    8. How will the existence of competition affect our goals, interests, strategies, and tactics in this negotiation?

  B. *Environment*
    1. Where should the negotiation take place?
    2. When will the negotiation take place? Have we checked the local calendar for conflicts, holidays, and other events that may affect negotiations?
    3. How long should we plan for the negotiation to last?

4. When should our team plan to arrive at the negotiation site? Will we arrive long enough in advance of negotiations to adjust to the surroundings and prepare for the talks?

5. When will we leave the negotiation site? Have we informed the other side of our arrival and departure plans?

6. Have we and the other side agreed on where the various negotiating rounds or sessions will take place?

7. Have we designated a home office person to "backstop" the negotiations? Have we agreed on a fixed time to communicate with the home office?

8. What language will be used in the negotiations?

9. Will an interpreter be used? Who will provide the interpretation?

10. What will the language of the contract be?

11. Have we made arrangements to brief the interpreter on the nature of the deal, the technical language, etc.?

C. *Our Negotiating Team*

1. Who will be the members of our negotiating team? Who will be its spokesperson?

2. Does our team have the right balance of functional skills, language ability, knowledge of the country, and negotiating experience?

3. Have specific responsibilities been allocated to individual team members for matters such as logistics, communications, note taking, etc.?

4. Has our team met to prepare its strategy, to formulate necessary draft documents, conduct simulations, etc.?

5. What specific authority does our team have to make commitments in the negotiation?

D. *The Other Side*

1. Are we certain we are dealing with the organization that can deliver what we want?

2. Are we dealing with the right persons or departments in that organization?

3. Are there other parties (especially the government) who should be at the negotiating table?

4. Are we fully informed of the other side's standing within the country and with its government?

E. *Information and Documentation*
   1. What information do we need about the other country, company, transactions, etc., before we begin negotiations? How will we obtain it?
   2. What information do we need about the members of the other team? How will we get that information? By what date do we need that information?
   3. What draft documents, slides, reports, and publications need to be prepared for the negotiations?
   4. What books, journals, reports, documents, and equipment need to accompany our team to the negotiation site?
   5. What local consultants and experts will we need to hire? Should they be present at the negotiations?

F. *Agenda*
   1. Have we agreed on an agenda with the other side?
   2. What are the items on the agenda?
   3. Does the agenda allow for surprises and topics we would rather not discuss?
   4. What items do we want to discuss first?

II. OPENING MOVES
   1. Have we fully introduced all the members of our team?
   2. Has the other side fully introduced all the members of its team?
   3. Do we know the identity of the leader of the other team and the roles played by its other members?
   4. What will the physical arrangements for the negotiations be?
   5. Have we spent sufficient time on getting to know the members of the other team?
   6. Will we make a comprehensive opening statement? What will it include?
   7. Have we reviewed the agenda with the other team?
   8. Do we have an accurate idea of the other team's negotiating

authority? Does the other team have an accurate idea of our negotiating authority?

III. NEGOTIATING DYNAMICS

1. Have we obtained sufficient information from the other side? Are we listening to them carefully? Do they know that we are listening carefully? What questions do we need to ask them?

2. Do we have a knowledge of the other side's culture? How will that culture affect the way we communicate with each other?

3. What are the principal issues in this negotiation? What order of importance does each have on a scale of 1 to 10?

4. What will be our strategy with respect to each issue? In what sequence will we address the issues?

5. At what point do we put forward our draft agreement as a basis for negotiation?

6. If the other side submits its draft agreement to us, how will we respond?

7. Are we watching for nonverbal, as well as verbal, forms of communication by the other side?

8. What social occasions with the other side will arise during the course of this negotiation? Are we sure we know how to respond and act appropriately according to local culture?

9. To what ideological factors must we be sensitive during the negotiations?

10. Who will bear the foreign exchange risk in this deal? If we are to bear it, how should we protect ourselves?

11. Have we examined the relevant exchange controls? How will they affect our deal? Will countertrade be a part of this transaction?

12. Has our team agreed to meet at the end of each day to review progress and plan for the next day's activities?

13. Have we prepared an adequate written record of the negotiations? What communication do we need to make with the other side after each negotiating session?

14. What other follow-up will be necessary? Who will be assigned to do it?

15. What options does the other side have to attain its goals and interests?
16. What options do we have to attain our goals and interests? Can we justify our various options according to objective criteria?
17. Are we sure that we really understand the other side's goals and interests?
18. Are we sure that the other side really understands our goals and interests?
19. Have we fully explained the nature of the transaction we are proposing? Do they fully understand the deal and its implications?

IV. ENDGAME

1. If we do make a deal, are we sure it will last?
2. What future events and trends might affect the agreement? How do we protect ourselves against these events?
3. How do we structure the agreement to minimize future uncertainties?
4. Is the deal balanced? Is it good for both sides?

Appendix B

Suggestions for Further Study

The following books and articles provide additional helpful information and advice for negotiating global deals generally and in specific areas.

GENERAL SOURCES

Binnendijk, Hans, ed. *National Negotiating Styles*. Washington, D.C.: Foreign Service Institute, U.S. Department of State, 1987.

Bryan, Robert M., and Peter C. Buck. "The Cultural Pitfalls in Cross-Border Negotiations." *Mergers and Acquisitions* 24, no. 2 (September/October 1989): 61–63.

Fadiman, Jeffrey. "Traveller's Guide to Gifts and Bribes." *Harvard Business Review* 64 (July/August 1986): 122–36.

Fisher, Glen. *International Negotiations: A Cross-Cultural Perspective*. Chicago: Intercultural Press, 1980.

Fisher, Roger, and William Ury. *Getting to Yes: Negotiating Agreement Without Giving In*. Boston: Houghton Mifflin, 1981.

Kapoor, Ashok. *Planning for International Business Negotiations*. Cambridge, Mass.: Ballinger, 1975.

Lax, David A., and James K. Sebenius. *The Manager as Negotiator: Bargaining for Cooperation and Competitive Gain*. New York: Free Press, 1986.

Posses, Frederick. *The Art of International Negotiation*. London: Business Books, Brookfield Publishing, 1978.

Raiffa, Howard. The Art and Science of Negotiation. Cambridge, Mass.: Harvard University Press, 1982.

Stoever, William A. *Renegotiations in International Business Trans-*

actions: *The Process of Dispute Resolution Between Multinational Investors and Host Societies.* Lexington, Mass.: Lexington Books, 1981.

Weiss, Stephen E., and William Stripp. *Negotiating with Foreign Business Persons: An Introduction for Americans with Propositions on Six Cultures.* Working Paper No. 1. New York: New York University Faculty of Business Administration, 1985.

Zartman, I. William, and Maureen R. Berman. *The Practical Negotiator.* New Haven: Yale University Press, 1982.

SPECIFIC AREAS

Algeria

Zartman, I. William, and Antonella Bassani. *Algerian Gas Negotiations.* PEW Case Studies, 103.0-C-86-J. Washington, D.C.: School of Advanced International Studies, Johns Hopkins University Press, 1986.

Argentina

Stiles, K. W. "Argentina's Bargaining with the IMF." *Journal of Inter-American Studies and World Affairs* 29, no. 3 (Autumn 1987): 55–86.

Asia

Borthwick, M. *Pacific Basin Approach to Trade Negotiations: A Study of Overlapping National Interests.* FAR-116-84. Washington, D.C.: U.S. Department of State, Office of External Research, 1985.

Chu, Chin-Ning. *The Asian Mind Game: Unlocking the Hidden Agenda of the Asian Business Culture: A Westerner's Survival Manual.* New York: Maxwell Macmillan International, 1990.

Graham, John L., and Ki Dong Kim. "Buyer-Seller Negotiations Around the Pacific Rim: Differences in Fundamental Exchange Processes." *Journal of Consumer Research* (June 1, 1988): 48ff.

Stone, Ray. "Negotiating in Asia." *Practicing Manager* 9, no. 2 (Australia, Autumn 1989): 36–39.

Australia

"Australia's Role in International Trade Negotiations." *Overseas Trading* 28, no. 23 (1976): 557–61.

Corbett, Hugh. "Australian Commercial Diplomacy in a New Era of Negotiation." *Australian Outlook* 26, no. 1 (1972), 3–17.

Brazil

Graham, John L. "Brazilian, Japanese, and American Business Negotiations." *Journal of International Business Studies* 14, no. 1 (Spring–Summer 1983): 44–66.

———. "The Influence of Culture on the Process of Business Negotiations: An Exploratory Study." *Journal of International Business Studies* 16, no. 1 (Spring 1985): 81–96. (Study of the United States, Japan, and Brazil.)

Hurrell, Andrew, and Ellen Felder. *U.S.-Brazilian Information Dispute.* PEW Case Studies, 122.0-E-88-J. Washington, D.C.: School of Advanced International Studies, Johns Hopkins University Press, 1988.

Rowland, W. S. "Foreign Investment in Brazil: A Reconciliation of Perspectives." *Journal of International Law and Economics* 14 (1979): 39–62.

Canada

Alder, Nancy J., and John L. Graham. "Cross-Cultural Interaction: The International Comparison Fallacy?" *Journal of International Business Studies* 20, no. 3 (Fall 1989): 515–37. (Study of Japanese, American, and Canadian Francophones and Canadian Anglophones.)

Bemmels, Brian, E. G. Fisher, and Barbara Nyland. "Canadian-American Jurisprudence on 'Good Faith' Bargaining." *Industrial Relations* 41, no. 3 (Canada, 1986): 596–620.

Grey, Rodney de C. "Negotiating About Trade and Investment in Services." In R. M. Stern, ed., *Trade and Investment in Services: Canada/U.S. Perspectives.* Toronto: Ontario Economic Council, 1985, 181–202.

Winham, Gilbert R. "Bureaucratic Politics and Canadian Trade Negotiations." *International Journal* 34, no. 1 (1979): 64–89.

The Caribbean

Radway, R. J. "Negotiating in the Caribbean Basin: Trade and Investment Contracts." *International Trade Law Journal* 4 (Winter 1978): 164–69.

Watson, H. A. "The Caribbean Basin, Its Subregions and Their Internal and International Social and Economic Dynamics." *International Trade Law Journal* 4 (Winter 1978): 197–213.

China

Chu, Chin-Ning. *The Chinese Mind Game: The Best Kept Trade Secret of the East.* Beaverton, Ore.: AMC Publishing, 1988.

Joy, Robert O. "Cultural and Procedural Differences That Influence Business Strategies and Operations in the People's Republic of China." *Advanced Management Journal* 54, no. 3 (Summer 1989): 29–33.

Kazuo, Ogura. "How the 'Inscrutables' Negotiate with the 'Inscrutables': Chinese Negotiating Treaties vis-à-vis the Japanese." *China Quarterly* 103 (September 1984): 530.

Macleod, Roderick K. *China, Inc.: How to Do Business with the Chinese.* New York: Bantam Books, 1988.

Pye, Lucien W. *Chinese Commercial Negotiating Style.* Cambridge, Mass.: Oelgeschlager, Gunn & Hain, 1982.

Pye, Lucien W., and S. R. Hendryx. "The China Trade: Making the Deal." *Harvard Business Review* 64, no. 4 (July/August 1986): 74–85.

Stewart, Sally, and Charles F. Keown. "Talking with the Dragon: Negotiating in the People's Republic of China." *Columbia Journal of World Business* 24, no. 3 (Fall 1989): 68–72.

Tung, Rosalie L. *U.S.-China Trade Negotiations.* New York: Pergamon Press, 1982.

Colombia

Kline, Harvey F. *The Coal of El Cerrejon: Dependent Bargaining and Colombian Policy Making.* University Park: Pennsylvania State University Press, 1987.

Developing Countries

Ghuari, Pervez N. "Negotiating International Package Deals: Swedish Firms and Developing Countries." Ph.D. diss., Acta Universitatis Upsaliensis, Studia Oeconomise Negotiorum, Uppsala, 1983.

Kapoor, Ashok. *Planning for International Business Negotiation.* Cambridge, Mass.: Ballinger, 1975.

Egypt

Quandt, William B. "Egypt: A Strong Sense of National Identity." In Hans Binnendijk, ed., *National Negotiating Styles*. Washington, D.C.: Foreign Service Institute, U.S. Department of State, 1987.

Europe

Altanny, David. "Europe 1992: Culture Crash." *Industry Week* 238, no. 19 (October 2, 1989): 13–20.

Bruce, Leigh. "North vs. South." *International Management* 44, no.5 (United Kingdom, May 1989): 20–26. (Cultural differences between the nations of northern and southern Europe.)

Campbell, Nigel C. G., John L. Graham, Alain Jolibert, and Hans Gunther Meissner. "Marketing Negotiations in France, Germany, the United Kingdom and the United States." *Journal of Marketing* 52, no. 2 (April 1988): 49–62.

Le Poole, Samfrits. "Negotiating with Clint Eastwood in Brussels." *Management Review* 78, no. 10 (October 1989): 58–60.

Zartman, I. William. *The Politics of Trade Negotiations Between Africa and the EEC: The Weak Confront the Strong*. Princeton: Princeton University Press, 1971.

France

Harrison, Michael M. "France: The Diplomacy of a Self-assured Middle Power." In Hans Binnendijk, ed., *National Negotiating Styles*. Washington, D.C.: Foreign Service Institute, U.S. Department of State, 1987.

Ghana

Tsilkata, Fui S. *Essays from the Ghana-Valco Renegotiations, 1982–1985*. Accra: Ghana Publishing, 1986.

India

Ghuari, Pervez N. "Negotiating with Firms in Developing Countries: Two Case Studies." *Industrial Marketing Management* 17, no. 1 (February 1988): 49–53. (Study of India and Nigeria.)

Kapoor, Ashok. "International Business—Government Negotiations: A Study in India." In I. William Zartman, ed., *The 50% Solution*. Garden City, N.Y.: Anchor Press, 1976, 430–51.

———. *International Business Negotiations: A Study in India*. New York: New York University Press, 1970.

Jamaica

Allen, Michael H. "The 1974 Jamaican Bauxite Negotiations as a Case Study in Bargaining." M.S. diss., University of the West Indies, Kingston, 1977.

Japan

Alder, Nancy J., and John L. Graham. "Cross-Cultural Interaction: The International Comparison Fallacy?" *Journal of International Business Studies* 20, no. 3 (Fall 1989): 515–37. (Study of Japanese, American, and Canadian Francophones and Canadian Anglophones.)

Aonuma, Y. "A Japanese Explains Japan's Business Style." *Across the Board* 18, no. 2 (February 1981): 41–50.

Graham, John L. "The Influence of Culture on the Process of Business Negotiations: An Exploratory Study." *Journal of International Business Studies* 16, no. 1 (Spring 1985): 81–96. (Study of the United States, Japan, and Brazil.)

Guittard, Stephen W. "Negotiating and Administering an International Sales Contract with the Japanese." *International Lawyer* 8 (1974): 822–31.

Guittard, Stephen W., and Sano Yoshihiro. *Smart Bargaining: Dealing with the Japanese.* New York: Harper & Row, 1989.

Hawrysh, Brian Mark, and Judith Lynne Zaichkowsky. "Cultural Approaches to Negotiations: Understanding the Japanese." *International Marketing Review* 7, no. 2 (United Kingdom, 1990): 28–42.

Herberger, Roy A. "Some Beliefs of Americans Can Lead to Wrong Conclusions." *The Nihon Keizai Shimbun Japan Economic Journal* (August 19, 1980): 24ff. (Article concerning American negotiation behavior written for a Japanese readership.)

March, Robert M. *The Japanese Negotiator: Subtlety and Strategy Beyond Western Logic.* Tokyo: Kodansha International, 1988.

McCreary, Don R. *Japanese-U.S. Business Negotiations: A Cross-Cultural Study.* New York: Praeger, 1986.

Rowland, Diana. *Japanese Business Etiquette: A Practical Guide to Business and Social Success with the Japanese.* New York: Warner Press, 1985.

Tung, Rosalie L. *Business Negotiating with the Japanese.* Lexington, Mass.: Lexington Books, 1984.

Zhang, Danian, and Kenji Kuroda. "Beware of Japanese Negotiating Style: How to Negotiate with Japanese Companies." *Northwestern Journal of International Law and Business* 10 (Fall 1989): 195–212.

Zimmerman, Mark. *How to Do Business with the Japanese.* New York: Random House, 1984.

Latin America

Jora, Joseph J., Clint E. Smith, and T. Frank Crigler. "Private Investment in Latin America: Renegotiating the Bargain." *Texas International Law Journal* 19 (Winter 1984): 3–32.

Leavy, James. "Negotiating a Common Law Guarantee in Latin America." *International Financial Law Review* 5, no. 7 (United Kingdom, July 1986): 32–34.

Mendosa, Eugene L. "How to Do Business in Latin America." *Purchasing World* 32, no. 7 (July 1988): 58–59.

Odell, John S. "Latin American Trade Negotiations with the United States." *International Organization* 34 (Spring 1980): 207–28.

Mexico

Bennett, Douglas C., and Kenneth E. Sharpe. "Agenda Setting and Bargaining Power: The Mexican State versus Transnational Corporations." *World Politics* 32, no. 1 (October 1979): 57–89.

Camp, Hope H., Jr. "A Role for U.S. Lawyers in Promoting Trade and Investment Between the United States and Mexico." *1988 Private Investors Abroad* 11, no. 1 (1988): 27.

Grayson, George W. "Mexico: A Love-Hate Relationship with North America." In Hans Binnendijk, ed., *National Negotiating Styles.* Washington, D.C.: Foreign Service Institute, U.S. Department of State, 1987.

Middle East

Alghanim, Kutayba. "How to Do Business in the Middle East." *Management Review* 65, no.8 (August 1976): 19–28.

Iqbal, Afzal. *The Prophet's Diplomacy: The Art of Negotiation as Conceived and Developed by the Prophet of Islam.* Cape Cod, Mass.: Claude Stark, 1975.

Rand, Edward J. "Learning to Do Business in the Middle East." *The Conference Board Record* 8, no.2 (February 1976): 49–51.

Sen, Sondra. "The Art of International Negotiating: Doing Business in the Middle East." *Art of Negotiating Newsletter* 11, no. 3 (December 1981).

Wright, P. "Doing Business in Islamic Markets." *Harvard Business Review* 59 (January/February 1981): 34.

Nigeria

Bierstecker, Thomas J. *Reaching Agreement with the IMF: The Nigerian Negotiations, 1983–1986.* PEW Case Studies, 205.0.-C-88-S. Los Angeles: School of International Relations, University of Southern California, 1988.

Ghuari, Pervez N. "Negotiating with Firms in Developing Countries: Two Case Studies." *Industrial Marketing Management* 17, no. 1 (February 1988): 49–53. (Study of India and Nigeria.)

Norway

Nye, D. A. "Formation of Contracts: The Law in Norway." *North Carolina Journal of International Law and Commercial Regulation* 12 (Spring 1987): 187–248.

The Philippines

Henze, L. J. "United States–Philippine Economic Relations and Trade Negotiations." *Asian Survey* 16, no. 4 (1976): 319–37.

Saudi Arabia

Lee, Eve. *The American in Saudi Arabia.* Yarmouth, Me.: Intercultural Press, 1980.

Mackey, Sandra. *The Saudis: Inside the Desert Kingdom.* Boston: Houghton Mifflin, 1987.

Mulligan, John W. "Saudi Risk Management: A Lesson in Irony." *Business Insurance* (August 17, 1981): 10ff.

Scandinavia

Haskel, Barbara G. "Disputes, Strategies and Opportunity Costs: The Example of Scandinavian Economic Market Negotiations." *International Studies Quarterly* 18, no. 2 (1974): 3–30.

South Africa

Johnson, Sandi, and Deon Herbst. *The Process of Negotiation: A Case Study of Wage Negotiations.* Pretoria: Human Sciences Research Council, 1986.

South Korea

Griffin, T. J. "Doing Business in Korea." *Washington State Business News* 43 (March 1989): 19–22.

Lee, Hyock Sup. "The U.S.-Korean Textile Negotiations of 1969–1972: A Case Study in the Relationship Between National Sovereignty and Economic Development." Ph.D. diss., University of Michigan, Ann Arbor, 1984.

Odell, John, David Land, and Tracy Tierney. *Bilateral Trade Negotiations Between South Korea and the United States.* PEW Case Studies, 129.0-G-88-S. Los Angeles: School of International Relations, University of Southern California, 1988.

Soviet Union

Beliaev, Edward, Thomas Mullen, and Betty Jane Punnett. "Understanding the Cultural Environment: U.S.-U.S.S.R. Trade Negotiations." *California Management Review* 27, no. 2 (Winter 1985): 100–112.

Gustafson, Thane. *Soviet Negotiating Strategy: The East-West Gas Pipeline Deal, 1980–1984.* Santa Monica: Rand Corporation, 1985.

Schmidt, Robert D. "Business Negotiations with the Soviet Union." In D. D. Newson, ed., *Private Diplomacy with the Soviet Union.* Lanham, Md.: University Press of America, 1987, 73–92.

U.S. Central Intelligence Agency, National Foreign Assessment Center. *Soviet Strategy and Tactics in Economic and Commercial Negotiations with the United States.* ER79-10276. Washington, D.C.: U.S. Government Printing Office, 1979.

Vlachoutsicos, Charalambos A. *What Business with the Soviets?: What, Who and How?* Working Paper. Boston: Division of Research, Harvard Business School, 1988.

———. "Where the Ruble Stops in Soviet Trade." *Harvard Business Review* 64 (September/October 1986): 82–86.

Sweden

Ghuari, Pervez N. "Negotiating International Package Deals: Swedish Firms and Developing Countries." Ph.D. diss., Acta Universitatis Upsaliensis, Studia Oeconomise Negotiorum, Uppsala, 1983.

Tanzania

Gulliver, P. H. *Disputes and Negotiations: A Cross-Cultural Perspective*. San Diego: Academic Press, 1979. (Includes a study of negotiation in the Arusha of Tanzania.)

United States

Campbell, Nigel C. G., John L. Graham, Alain Jolibert, and Hans Gunther Meissner. "Marketing Negotiations in France, Germany, the United Kingdom, and the United States." *Journal of Marketing* 52, no. 2 (April 1988): 49–62.

Graham, John L. "The Influence of Culture on the Process of Business Negotiations: An Exploratory Study." *Journal of International Business Studies* 16, no. 1 (Spring 1985): 81–96. (Study of the United States, Japan, and Brazil.)

Graham, John L., and R. A. Herberger. "Negotiators Abroad — Don't Shoot from the Hip: Cross-Cultural Business Negotiations." *Harvard Business Review* 61 (July/August 1983): 160–68.

Herberger, Roy A. "Some Beliefs of Americans Can Lead to Wrong Conclusions." *The Nihon Keizai Shimbun Japan Economic Journal* (August 19, 1980) 24ff. (Article concerning American negotiation behavior written for a Japanese readership.)

Notes

CHAPTER 2

1. Adrian Furham and Stephen Bochner, *Culture Shock: Psychological Reactions to Unfamiliar Environments* (New York: Methuen, 1986).
2. For information on the Zaire negotiation, I am indebted to an unpublished manuscript, "Mobil Oil Corporation and Petro Zaire: Post-Nationalization Negotiations in Zaire," by Ann Williams.
3. For a detailed discussion of this tripartite analysis, see I. William Zartman and Maureen R. Berman, *The Practical Negotiator* (New Haven: Yale University Press, 1982).
4. In *Getting to Yes: Negotiating Agreement Without Giving In* (Boston: Houghton Mifflin, 1981), Roger Fisher and William Ury advise negotiators to develop their BATNA—Best Alternative to a Negotiated Agreement.
5. See, for example, ibid., and Zartman and Berman, *Practical Negotiator*.

CHAPTER 3

1. For a slightly different but more detailed analysis of the impact of culture on negotiation, see Stephen E. Weiss, *Negotiating with Foreign Business Persons: An Introduction for Americans with Propositions on Six Cultures* (New York: New York University Faculty of Business Administration, Working Paper No. 1, February 12, 1985).
2. John L. Graham and R. A. Herberger, "Negotiators Abroad—Don't Shoot from the Hip: Cross-Cultural Business Negotiations," *Harvard Business Review* 61 (July/August 1983): 160–83.

3. Geert Hofstede, *Culture's Consequences: International Differences in Work-Related Values* (Newbury Park, Calif.: Sage Publications, 1980), 151.

CHAPTER 6

1. For a discussion of this case, see David A. Lax and James K. Sebenius, *The Manager as Negotiator: Bargaining for Cooperation and Competitive Gain* (New York: Free Press, 1986), 354–55.

CHAPTER 8

1. For an interesting discussion of this principle and the problem of sustaining agreements, consult David A. Lax and James K. Sebenius, *The Manager as Negotiator: Bargaining for Cooperation and Competitive Gain* (New York: Free Press, 1986), 279–89.
2. Ibid., 281–82.

Index

"Administrative fees," 50, 81
Africa, 52, 93, 112, 117. *See also names of countries*
Agendas, organizational and personal, 100–101
Agreement: draft, 15, 35–41; form of, 66–67; inductive or deductive method in achieving, 68. *See also* Contract
Algeria, 86, 175
Arab countries, 48–49, 50, 74, 79–80. *See also* names of countries; Islamic law
Arbitration, international, 128–30; ad hoc and institutional, 129
Argentina, 175
Asia, 47, 52, 175. *See also* names of countries
Attitude, negotiating, 60–63. *See also* Negotiating style
Australia, 121–22, 175–76
Authority, 17, 68–69

Bad faith, 27
Bankruptcy laws, 121–22

Banks, as information sources, 54, 88, 119
Bargaining position, in negotiations, 15, 38, 40, 60–61, 66–67. *See also* Authority; Clout
Barter, 141–42. *See also* Countertrade
Body language, 20, 42
Brazil, 47, 48, 176
Bribery, 101
Bureaucracies, foreign. *See* Foreign bureaucracy(-ies)
Buyback. *See* Compensation

Calvo doctrine, 76
Canada, 176
Caribbean, 176–77
Checklist, Global Deal Negotiation, 169–173
China, 7, 30, 34, 66–67, 69, 93, 96, 108, 177
Clout, of other negotiating team, 94–95. *See also* Bargaining position
Colombia, 177

Communication, 42–53, 151;
nonverbal, 20, 42; cultural dif-
ferences in style, 44, 47–50,
55–56, 64–65; failure of, 45;
direct or indirect methods, 64–
65; ideology and, 75
Compensation (or buyback),
142–43, 145
"Compensation ratio," 143–44
Computer spreadsheet, for draft
and counterdraft, 40
Conceptualization phase of negotiations, 25, 26, 27
Concessions, 95
Confidentiality, 82. See also Secrecy
Conflict, 19, 29, 40, 64–65, 86
Conflicts of interest, and local
legal advisers, 120
Consensus, group, 68–69, 90
Consumer goods, 78, 80, 81
Context of negotiations, 58, 69–
70
Continuation of discussions, 15
Contract(s), 6; language of, 33;
as negotiating goal, 59–60,
65, 66, 149; form of, 66–67;
and state corporations, 109,
110; and foreign laws, 114,
116–17; legal pluralism and,
122, 123; arbitration clause,
128, 129–30; renegotiating,
147–63; instability of, 148–
49, 159; enforcement of, 149;
sanctity of, 149, 155–56, 157,
158. See also Draft agreement
Corruption, 101–2
Counterdraft, 39–40

Counterpurchase, 141–42
Countertrade, 140–46; types of,
141–43; negotiating, 143–46
Cultural differences, 2–3, 5, 45–
53, 175–83; in communication
style, 47–50, 55–56; effect on
negotiations, 58–70
Cultural groups, 52–53
Cultural stereotypes, 55–56, 65–
66
Culture, 3, 5, 42–71; differences
in, 2–3, 5, 45–53; defined,
45; sources of information on,
54–55, 57; effect on negotiations, 58–70
Culture shock, 9, 11, 17
Currency, 6, 131–46; convertibility of, 132–46; movable
money, 132–37; and foreign
exchange risk, 132–37; immovable money, 137–46; and
countertrade, 140–46

Deadlines, 51, 58
"Deal, The": as contract or relationship, 59–60, 65, 66, 153,
164; as a partnership, 149
Details, working out, 25, 26
Developing countries, 17, 75,
93, 123, 177; in negotiation
with multinational corporations, 15, 39–40; and countertrade, 140, 143–44, 145
Discrimination, against foreigners, 104, 123–30
Documentation, of negotiation
process, 99

Documents, 25, 35–41, 99. See also Contract(s); Draft (or model) agreement
Draft (or model) agreement, 15, 35–41; purposes of, 36–37; risks of, 37–38; other side's, 39–41; and counterdraft, 39–40; and discussion of principles, 40–41

Eastern Europe, 80–81, 109
Egypt, 18, 64, 74, 79–80, 81, 110, 178
Electronic negotiation, 19–21
Embassies: as information sources, 54, 78, 89, 119; U.S., 125–26
Emotionalism, degree of, 65–66, 167–68
Environment. See Negotiating environment
Europe, 178. See also names of countries
European currency unit (ECU), 136
Exchange control systems, 137–38, 139
Exchange rates, 132–37. See also Currency
Exposure netting, 135–36

Failure, risk of, 7, 27, 45
First names, use of, 43, 63
Flexibility, importance of, 166
Foreign bureaucracy(-ies), 5–6, 84–102; approaches to dealing with, 85–91; multiplicity of, 86; identifying appropriate branch of, 87–88, 89; and the other negotiating team, 91–102; and second channel, 92–93
Foreign Corrupt Practices Act, 101
Foreign government(s), 5–6, 103–13; challenges in dealing with, 103–13; as a "black box," 104, 105–20; and "the squeeze," 104, 120–23; and "hometown justice," 104, 123–30; role in negotiations, 106–13, 124–27, 149; and national priorities, 107–8; pervasiveness of, 108–10; and contracts, 109, 110; and sovereign immunity, 111; as ghost negotiator, 124–26
Foreign investment, 79–80
Foreign laws, 6, 103–4, 113–20; challenges in dealing with, 113–20; as a "black box," 104, 113–15, 118; and "the squeeze," 104, 120–23; and "hometown justice," 104, 123–30; and contracts, 114, 116–17; and foreign legal advice, 118–20; bankruptcy, 121–22
Formality, degree of, 63–64, 166; and use of first name, 43, 63
France, 68, 74, 96, 113–14, 116, 178

Ghana, 178
Global Deal Negotiation Checklist, 169–73

"Globalization" of business, 1–2, 103
Goal(s), negotiating, 169; contract or relationship as, 59–60, 65, 66, 149, 153, 164; of foreign governments, 111–12
Government corporations, 109–10, 111–12, 124. *See also* Foreign government(s)

History of a culture, learning, 54, 62, 77
"Home court" advantage, 11–15
"Hometown justice," 104, 123–30
Hospitality, 11, 12. *See also* Socializing

Ideology, 5, 72–83; elements of, 73–74; and making the deal, 74–76; rules for dealing with, 76–82; personal, organizational, and national, 79; gaps between reality and, 80–81; as positive force, 83
India, 178
Individual rights, 75, 76
Indonesia, 118
Inductive *vs.* deductive methods, in negotiation, 68
Instability: risk of, 6, 147–49, 160; of negotiating team, 99–100; contractual, 148–49, 150
Interest/finance charges, Muslim prohibition of, 50, 81
Interests: determining, 61–63, 167; focusing on, 80

Interpretation, simultaneous *vs.* consecutive, 31
Interpreter, using an 30–33
Interruptions, cultural differences and, 48–49
Introductions, at negotiating table, 94–95
Islamic law, 24, 50, 81

Jamaica, 179
Japan and the Japanese, 50–51, 69, 83, 90, 105–6, 179–80; communication style, 47–49, 64–65; relationship as negotiating goal, 59–60, 149; ideology of, 73–74, 76; team leadership in, 96, 97; role of government in negotiations, 105–6; value of yen, 133–34, 150
Jargon, 32, 45–46, 75
Jet lag, 13
Joint ventures, 7, 18, 40–41, 53, 75, 107, 108, 111–12; equity, 139

Land rights, 117–18
Language, 28–33; and use of interpreter, 30–33; of the contract, 33
Latin America, 48, 65–66, 74, 76, 96, 180. *See also* names of countries
Laws, foreign. *See* Foreign laws
Lawyers: as negotiators, 34; foreign, 118–20
Leadership, team, 34, 95–97

Learning another culture: importance of, 13, 16–17, 18, 19, 20, 22, 50–51, 53–58, 62, 77–78; resources for, 54–55, 57
Legal issues, 34. See also Foreign laws
Legal system, 6; foreign, 104, 113–20; and foreign legal advice, 118–20
Letters of credit, 139, 145, 161
Letters of intent, 25, 27, 114
Linkage, 161
Location. See Site selection; Setting

Mexico, 47, 62, 180
Middle East, 21, 23, 24, 50, 180–81
Monetary systems, 6, 131–46; and foreign exchange risk, 132–37; and countertrade, 140–46. See also Currency
Morita, Akio, 56
"Most favored customer clause," 145
"Most favored nation treatment," 125
Multinational corporations, 15, 36, 39–40, 67
Multiple money, 6

Names: first, 43, 63; and introductions, 94–95
Nasser, Gamal, 79–80
Nationalism, 75, 76, 81
Nationalization, 19, 83, 126, 127

Negotiating environment, 5, 9–41, 169–70; site selection, 10–21, 82; time factors, 21–27; and phase of negotiations, 27; and language, 28–33; and negotiating team, 33–35; and drafts, 35–41
Negotiating style, 5, 47–48, 59, 70–71, 112–13; formal and informal, 43, 63–64, 166; win/win or win/lose attitude, 60–63; and emotionalism, 65–66, 167–67; inductive vs. deductive, 68; Type A and Type B, 70–71
Negotiating team, 33–35, 68–69, 170–71; size of, 33–34, 69, 93; spokesperson of, 34, 95; preparation by, 34–35, 165, 169–71; task allocation on, 35; and consensus, 68–69; and foreign bureaucracies, 91–102; other side's, 91–102; introductions at negotiating table, 94–95; leadership of, 95–97; stability of, 97–100; agenda of, 100–101; foreign government's role on, 108; Checklist for, 169–73
Nigeria, 22, 52–53, 181
Nixon, Richard, 67
"No," meaning of, 47, 57
Nonverbal communication, 20, 42
Norway, 181

Offsetting transactions, 135–36, 142

O'Neill, Thomas ("Tip"), 138
Organizational factors, 57–58

Pace of negotiations, 22–23, 24, 58
Payoffs, 101–2
Performance bond, 161
"Performance requirements," 124
Personality factors, 56–57, 59, 63–64, 66, 69
Personal style, 63–64, 70–71. *See also* Personality factors
Philippines, 181
Pluralism, legal and political, 121, 122–23
Power balance, in negotiations, 15, 40, 60–61, 66–67
Prenegotiation, 25–27, 169–71
Preparation for negotiations, 34–35, 165, 169–71. *See also* Learning another culture
Principles: discussion of, 40–41; agreement on, 66, 68
Priorities, national, 107–8
Private investment, 75–76, 79–80
Products, adapting, 50–51
Profits, 75, 76
Property, conceptions of, 116
Protectionism, 140

Question, as negotiating tool, 61–62

Reciprocity, principle of, 62
Relationship, 16, 166–67; as goal of deal, 59–60, 65, 66, 153, 164

Renegotiation, 137, 147–63; contractual instability and, 148–49; rejection and, 150–57, 161; types of, 151–57; approaches to, 157–59; preventing, 159–62
Resources, information, 54–55, 57, 77–78, 88–89, 119
Respect, showing, 32–33, 166
Risk(s): of instability, 6, 147–49, 160; of failure, 7, 27, 45; of draft agreement, 37–38; political, 126–27, 139; foreign exchange, 132–37; allocating, 134–35, 160
Risk taking, 69–70
Role playing, in preparation, 35

Sadat, Anwar, 79, 80
Saudi Arabia, 32, 140, 142, 181
Scandinavia, 181
Secrecy, 62. *See also* Confidentiality
Setting for negotiations, 47, 48–49. *See also* Site selection
Silences, meaning of, 47–48
Simulated negotiations, 35
Site selection, 10–21, 82; own territory, 11–15; opponent's territory, 16–18; neutral territory, 18–19; and technological advances, 19–21; symbolic value of, 16; alternating sites, 17–18
Slang and jargon, avoiding, 32, 45–46, 75
Socializing, 11, 12–13, 20, 47, 91, 166–67

South Africa, 181
South Korea, 182
Sovereign immunity, 111
Soviet Union, 67, 82, 87, 121, 182
Special drawing right (SDR), 136
Spokesperson, on negotiating team, 34. *See also* Team leader
State Department, as information source, 54
State-owned corporations, 109–10, 111–12, 124
Stereotypes, cultural, 55–56, 65–66
Style. *See* Negotiating style
Subsidies, state, 111
Sudan, 64, 86, 98, 117–18, 119
Sweden, 182

Tanzania, 183
Taxation, 6, 119, 123
Team leader, 34, 95–97
Technology, as aid to negotiation, 19–21
Technology transfer, 139
Third World. *See* Developing countries
Time, 7–8, 15, 21–27; time differences, 23–24; cultural differences in perception of, 15, 22, 65; sensitivity to, 65
Trade, to avoid exchange controls, 140–43

Trading company, 141, 146
Translator. *See* Interpreter
Tribal law, 117
Trust, 66
Turf issues, 5, 10–21. *See also* Negotiating environment; Site selection
Type A and Type B negotiators, 70–71

Ultimatums, 15
United Nations Convention on the Recognition and Enforcement of Foreign Arbitral Awards, 130
Units of account, 136

Video teleconferencing, 19–21
Visas, 14

Waiver, as renegotiation, 158
Walk-away point, 35, 102
"Westernization," 56–57
Win/win *vs.* win/lose negotiating attitude, 60–63
Worker participation in management, 81, 82

Yamani, Zaki, 56
Yen, value of, 133–34, 150

Zaire, 17, 22, 83, 158–59